THE HUMAN, ESSENTIAL IDENTITY

By Julian Hamer

Dedicated to my beautiful wife Ellen

THE HUMAN, ESSENTIAL IDENTITY
Direct Experience of the Intangible Significance of Existence through the Immediate Engagement of the Human Essence

By Julian Hamer

Contents

Introduction

It is from the perspective of our own intrinsic existence that natural circumstances are recognized for the authenticity of their original condition. They are discovered in the state in which they exist before they are humanly appraised and evaluated upon the particulars of their physical appearances.

Consequently, it is hardly surprising that, on the strength of an original perspective towards existence, a familiarity with the authentic condition of things should be established. Theories and constructions concerning phenomena are thrown into a rather harsh light when circumstances are experienced directly for their legitimate significance. For which reason, having immediate experience of the condition of things as they exist intrinsically reveals the shortcomings of conjecture and supposition and one finds little distinction between the abstract approach towards life, and belief, except perhaps in the extent of the scholarship.

The purpose of this exploration of the neglected qualitative dimension of existence is not to deny the significance of the material appearance or of physical properties but to demonstrate that an exclusively materialistic perspective will only reveal information of a one-sided nature. It is not that the materially founded data is erroneous, but in terms of essential existence, physical appearances are not recognized as intrinsically

1

extant. A table, for example, also possesses the significance of its conception, manufacture and the volition of the craftsman who made it, without which it would not exist. The exclusively physical perspective is one that is inevitably restricted to the obvious details and properties. Accordingly, in terms of realizing the greater significance, it is the shallowness and imperceptiveness of the observer that is at fault. Indeed, from an exclusively materialistic point of view, only the appearances of phenomena are considered pertinent while the intrinsic existence and intangible qualitative dimension are marginalized. Therefore, it is small wonder that humanity frequently maintains only a shallow and superficial understanding towards existence.

The inclusion of the qualitatively expressive dimension of existence to our world-view reduces blatant appearances to modest relevance, but it does not denounce their existence. The problem is that materialistic, Western philosophy insists that the appearance is the sole significance of the phenomenon. Nevertheless, a philosophy founded upon evidence solely derived from the tangible condition of things is an erroneous abstraction that is misleadingly simplistic. In fact, exclusive materialism does not stand up to even casual scrutiny because we constantly recognize physically elusive conditions throughout everyday experience. Therefore, if the material appearances and their physical properties are considered and assumed to encompass the entirety of existence, the resulting amalgamation fails to correspond to our experiential knowledge of life because it is void of qualitative significance. Consequently, either people are imagining the existence of the qualitative significance of things or materialistic Western philosophy that excludes essential significances is fundamentally at fault.

Indeed, missing from materialistic, Western philosophy is the profundity of the intrinsic identity and qualitative dimension of existence. The significance of qualities is minimized because they do not possess physical representation, and they are further excluded from our assessment of life through lack of tangible evidence. However, qualities are known to exist through immediate experience, and even though their occurrence is not considered significantly pertinent, all things possess qualitative, existential expression as well as material evidence. Indeed, the qualitative distinction of a phenomenon is of enormous relevance because it reveals the authentic, intrinsic identity as opposed to the merely shallow semblance that is the consequence of an exclusively material view.

However, the discovery of the significance of the qualitative dimension of existence requires a different cognitive approach than our conventional practice. The appearance of things is obvious but we discern the intangible dimension of phenomena through direct, experiential engagement. Furthermore, the immanent

3

condition wherein qualities reside remains intellectually remote because it requires immediate apprehension in order to be known.

Recognizing the inadequacy of conventional cognition whereby phenomena are examined and evaluated upon the evidence of their physical appearances, we postpone our usual approach. Rationale and emotional appraisal, references to established convictions and preconceptions, are set aside and the phenomenon is engaged experientially, and immediately. Thereby, we discover that reliance upon abstract rationalism and analytical deduction pales beside the efficacy of direct engagement. That is to say, through immediate, cognitive engagement we no longer require an intermediary interpretation of phenomena but now things are directly engaged and discovered for their intrinsic condition of existence.

Confronting the object immediately, removes evaluative bias and the phenomena is experienced directly. Further, when a phenomenon is immediately encountered instead of merely abstractly evaluated, we find that we engage it from the perspective of our own essential existence. That is to say, the human being is no longer misidentified with the corporeal, but found to exist in a similarly essential condition to the object of our observation. Thereupon, it is further discovered that the authentic, human identity is independently extant. Consequently, phenomena can be engaged directly from

4

an essential perspective and discerned for the similarly intrinsic significances.

We recognize the inherently limited scope of a perspective that solely evaluates the physical properties of phenomena and determines their identities upon that basis. Finding that materialistic, Western philosophy only concedes value to the material condition, we explore experiential engagement as a point of view, whereby the intrinsic nature of existence may be revealed.

Thereby, we discover that direct cognition presents us with definitive knowledge concerning existence because it deals with the essential significance of phenomena. Thus, the qualitative dimension is immediately and experientially engaged from the perspective of the authentic identity of the human being and an intangible condition is discovered that is in every respect, profound. Subsequently, the full impact of immediate engagement through the aegis of the human, essential identity reveals a hitherto unappreciated dimensionality of existence, in the face of which, the exclusively materialistic perspective is recognized as both meager and deceptive.

1. IMMEDIATE EXPERIENCE

The human, essential identity recognizes itself to be authentic through direct, experiential cognition. The incorporeal singularity is the agency of the human constitution that is able to recognize intangible realities and discern their intrinsic identities. It also discovers its own authenticity through immediate experience.

One would imagine that upon the strength of even a very cursory consideration of the human condition it would behoove us to explore the situation of our existence directly, for ourselves rather than merely rely upon the established perspective of another authority. It is, after all our own status that is being adjudicated. But perhaps entrenched positions are sufficient for us, particularly if they can be reduced to a choice between merely one apparent conviction, over another.

The current antagonism between the Neo-Darwinist and the creationist or, the philosophical materialist and those convinced of an alternative realm to the physical, is a case in point. However, the crux of the matter under discussion here has more pertinently to do with the intrinsic human condition than an attempt to establish a position or promote a particular belief system.

Deduction works most efficiently with quantifiable, physically justified properties. The intellect manipulates ideas remotely from their context in an attempt to understand existence. In order to facilitate their management, reason endeavors to quantify known and universally accepted conditions, even those without physical form. That failing, intangibles are summarily dismissed as insignificant. Authentic existence, through the selectivity of the materialistic approach, is superseded by a rational construct that appears to make good sense even though it is abstractly reasoned. But any intellectual formulation that attempts to replace an authentic condition represents only a shadow of the original.

It is assumed that intangible phenomena are judiciously evaluated solely through our intellectual capacity. Consequently, experiential knowledge of an incorporeal dimension to phenomena is considered subjective because it remains beyond the capacity of indirect deduction to evaluate. There is no physically justified data and reason cannot abstractly authenticate the existence of intangibles. The credibility of intangible values remains dubious because they cannot be conceptually identified but have to be directly experienced in order to be endorsed. The intellectual concept remains remote from the actual event because it is abstractly conceived, but values, qualities and intrinsic identities are qualified not through rationalism but by direct engagement. Their significance is justified through immediate experience.

Abstract conceptualization is a cerebral function that is incommensurable with cognition through immediate, experiential engagement. The former is indirect while experience is immediate. Immediacy involves the encounter of a circumstance in its extant condition. The cerebral approach cannot assimilate intangible significances and convinces us that definitive knowledge concerning the incorporeal remains beyond our human capacity to justify and consequently, the most persuasively argued, materialistic position and the one most logically reasoned, is adopted by default.

This would be tolerable if the proponents of the exclusively materialistic approach to cognition were to append the caveat that theirs is merely the most reasonable policy towards an essentially unsolvable conundrum. While intangibles cannot be definitively argued through reasoned exposition, they are recognized as extant, experientially. But even in the face of obvious contradictions, the intellect is presumed to be without limitation and its authority is considered the final arbiter of authenticity by materialistic, Western philosophy. The conviction that existence is identified exclusively with the physical, is adopted by consensus. Meanwhile, intangible but experientially acknowledged realities, are excluded from consideration. The materialistic position is defended as inviolate even though the cognitive capacity of the intellect is exclusively limited to evaluating physical appearances.

In order that something be known originally, it must be immediately engaged through the agency of the human, intrinsic identity. However, increasingly, the human being is imagined to be solely organic. The brain is thought to be the quintessence of human singularity. While on the face of it, it matters less whether we imagine the human being to be corporeal or incorporeal, understating the human, essential identity has enormous cognitive significance. Direct cognition requires the perspective of the human, essential identity in order to immediately engage reality. Essential significances are only discernible because the human quintessence inhabits the same condition of existence as the intrinsic identity of all other phenomenal appearances.

The direct experience of the intangible significance of existence is a cognitive practice that requires immediate engagement through the aegis of the human, essential identity. The direct apprehension of phenomena involves an undistracted encounter whereby both cerebral activity and sentimental influence are restrained. Thereby, the essential existence of an object is discovered for its authenticity through immediate experience. Whether it be the recognition of one's own essential identity, the inherent individuality of another or the intrinsic nature of the phenomenal-world, the approach must be both immediate and unsullied by preconception or sentimental preference. A phenomenon is encountered by the authentic, human identity in its elemental and original condition. Further, it will be found that knowledge through direct cognition is corroborative. There exists only one reality.

A qualitative discrepancy is revealed between knowledge achieved through direct cognition and the conclusions of abstract rationalism or sentimental evaluation. While we experience intangibles directly and, consequently, know them for their significance they are demeaned as trivial by the intellect. Reason is unable to deduce and justify the existence of physically insubstantial factors through abstract thinking, and incorporeal significances are considered of marginal importance.

Rational methodology is a cerebral practice that involves calculation and evaluation but it does not experience. The brain functions abstractly and cannot definitively evaluate the existence of phenomena that exist intangibly and must be experientially justified. It evaluates the attributes of physical properties very well, but it cannot assess intangibles because they have no material existence and consequently no manageable data. Yet, the qualitative value and essential identity of things are recognized as authentic without its agency. Through the human, cognitive capacity of immediate engagement, definitive intelligence concerning the intrinsic existence of phenomena is immanently conspicuous.

Reason assesses objects indirectly. It associates an observation with previous concepts. Thus, it evaluates a phenomenon not upon its originality but through comparison, searching the memory for the analogous. It works abstractly to try to match new information with previous concepts and compensating for any discrepancy through systematic imagination that is, ideally, logical. Compared to direct engagement, conventional rationalism, inherently influenced by materialistic preference, is recognized as a cogitative practice inevitably remote from the event. It requires that information be distilled from physical phenomena and upon that restricted basis the materialist establishes a distorted world-view composed exclusively of superficial information.

Not content with the authority of our personal concepts we also attempted to decipher a situation based upon the established perspectives of recognized authority even though our actual scholarship of them often remains scant and our application remote from the original context. We consult what we understand of the positions of Darwin, Kierkegaard, Sartre or a pundit of our particular subject area and preference. Exhaustive study of the positions of the experts, whether specialists of science, religion or philosophy, merely offers us additional opinions that may yet remain to be authenticated. The scholarly approach may satisfy us, and we may adopt those ideas that we agree with, but we never really know anything indisputably because the cerebral approach itself is indirect and abstract regardless of how elastic, imaginative and convincing an argument may be. We find that we have not even remotely arrived at definitive knowledge in spite of all our research. There is, therefore, little autonomy of thought in merely maintaining an adoptive position.

Abstract rationalism is of less pertinence if we wish to discover what something is definitively. Clearly, the indirect approach is limited, but we assume that it is our highest cognitive capacity. This is further exacerbated by a materialistic prejudice which convinces us that the extent of knowledge revealed by the intellect is all there is and that only phenomena accessible to our physical senses are verifiable as authentic.

Definitive knowledge remains remote to deductive reason by virtue of the oblique manner of cerebral functioning and because abstract thinking deals only with certain particular and restricted aspects of a phenomenon. It is compelling to believe that the intellect is the ultimate cognitive authority because we respect the convincing manner in which it functions. But it is exclusively limited to certain values of information. It cannot fathom intangibles but must have physical properties of some kind to work on. Consequently, there exists a conflict. The human being experiences the reality of values and qualities that have no physical presence while the intellect remains unable to comprehend them.

The proposal offered here is that the intangible values that we know through immediate experience and recognize as qualities, values and intrinsic identities, exist as significant realities and determine the authentic and essential identity of phenomena. They are as real as easily discernible, physical properties. Qualitative significances reveal the authentic existence of things while scrutiny of the appearance of a phenomenon merely evaluates the blatant material attributes. We are drawing attention to the qualitative dimension discarded by materialistic, Western philosophy and emphasizing the incorporeal inherence of things that epitomize their real identity. This requires the recognition of the inherent limitation of reasoned exposition, belief and sentiment, as the arbiters of authenticity, and the exploration of a manner of cognition that is not interpretative but experiences and knows a phenomenon immediately. Thus, existence is directly engaged without the filter of the intellect or the feeling nature.

Direct cognition is not a philosophy nor a religion. Everyone practices it without being aware that they are using a scarcely explored manner of intelligence. It is experienced vaguely and unknowingly. It is deemed by materialistic philosophy to be an unreliable emotional activity, an arbitrary sixth sense or an aberration of the brain. Intellectual dexterity is considered unrivaled, while intelligence through the immediate engagement of existence is dismissed as unfounded. Cognition, independent of the intellect, is associated with dubious, mystical practices and subjectively established information that cannot be readily assessed or justified.

Our intention is to acknowledge the validity of

intangible values as authentic in their own right and cease marginalizing them as irrational or attributing their recognition to a brain function. The brain cannot calculate intangibles. The recognition of incorporeal significance is achieved through the similarly incorporeal identity of the human being. The intellect functions indirectly with tangibles, while it manages intangibles; only as hypotheticals. It may acknowledge them and attempt to calculate them through quantification, but the brain can never definitively evaluate something that is essentially incorporeal.

The direct approach gains validity through engagement. The intellect will predictably deride immediate cognition because unknown unless directly practiced, it does not involve cerebral activity. The materialistic approach is convinced of the exclusive significance of physical properties and denies the existence of incorporeal reality. It is extraordinary how entrenched this position is, particularly since, in everyday life intangibles must be constantly addressed otherwise the individual would be promptly deemed insane. Inquiry, contrary to previously established convictions, is not even attempted by the staunch materialist. A manner of cognition that may yield definitive knowledge is dismissed as unfounded because it is incomprehensible to the mentality that is convinced of the fallibility of an exclusively intellectual approach. The materialist retreats to the safety of pre-established concepts that are predictably of someone else's founding and merit, and seldom of one's own inception or discovery.

Immediate cognition by the human, essential identity engages phenomena originally. It experiences the qualitative inherence and recognizes their significance as identities and, thereby, immediately knows their authenticity. It postpones analysis and intellectual evaluation, setting aside sentiment and preference. It engages a situation as it exists elementally and endorses qualitative distinctions through direct experience discovering, thereby the authentic identity of phenomena.

2. INTRINSIC SIGNIFICANCE

Direct cognition enables the human, essential identity to experience phenomena immediately and know things as they really are. Conventionally, we think about something and endeavor to assess its nature through our faculty of reason. The latter activity is necessarily abstract because it is remote from an immediate engagement. It is an oblique, cognitive practice by virtue of its indirectness. When the human quintessence experiences a situation, uninfluenced by what we assume we already know concerning it or that which we can decipher from its physical properties through reason, our subsequent knowledge is of a unique caliber. We have engaged the phenomenon directly and consequently, through our immediate approach we have experienced it in reality. We now know it for its intrinsic identity and as it exists authentically because we encounter it without forethought or prejudice. We experience the intrinsic nature of its identity, recognizing it immediately for what it is, in present timing, through direct encounter. We evaluate the phenomenon not merely by its superficial appearance but we engage it essentially.

When the human, intrinsic identity engages a phenomenon immediately and nothing obscures a direct, experiential encounter of its actuality, the thing is known for what it is. Direct cognition reveals the untarnished authenticity of the object unsullied by preconceptions and interpretation.

Direct cognition is necessary because the cerebral evaluation of exclusively physical properties does not involve the essential reality. Consequently, knowledge established exclusively upon the material appearance, is incomplete. Immediacy is a condition that cannot be understood or discovered through reason and deduction. It must be directly experienced in order to be known. Phenomena are either immediately engaged or their intrinsic condition remains elusive. Analysis and reasoned exposition are ideal functions for determining the physicality of phenomenal appearances and the imagination endeavors to explore possible relationships and further, similar information is assessed in order to compound a position and discover if a hypothetical evaluation is justified. But intrinsic identities are elusive to reason because they are incorporeal and the intellect only convincingly manages tangibly accessible data. Intangible factors may be implied, but it is not certain if they actually exist or are feigned. They cannot be definitely identified through abstract rationalism.

Direct cognition is achieved when the human, cerebral activity is voluntarily suspended and sentimental responses are postponed along with preconceptions, in order that a phenomenon can be experienced immediately and known for what it is. The human intrinsicality meets an object assuming no prior intelligence concerning it. It is experienced for its authenticity because no mental or emotional activity is permitted to superimpose an explanation or to gainsay its identity. The human essence engages it directly. It is experienced immediately in the condition of its authentic existence.

Thus, we recognize the existence of two cognitive approaches. The one is an indirect, cerebral practice that reasons and evaluates information concerning the material appearances of phenomena, while the other engages an object of interest not abstractly, but immediately. The human intellect evaluates the material world cerebrally but only the human, essential identity knows phenomena directly for their intrinsic significance. The incorporeal, yet essential identity, which is the human singularity of existence, recognizes the same intrinsicality of nature that essentially comprises other phenomena and, through immediacy, engages them in the condition of their authentic existence

The experience of the real through direct cognition builds within the human being a comparative sense of what the actual is like. Thereafter, no abstractly conceived construct, hypothesis or belief system is sufficient. Reality is known through first-hand involvement and, consequently, indirectly surmised interpretations of existence fall short of experiential knowledge. They appear to us to be beside the point, while material appearances are revealed as consequent upon the essential condition and recognized as only superficially, representative.

The materialistic perspective must assuredly fail over time because the results and conclusions of a world-view that is exclusively physical are untenable in comparison to direct, experiential knowledge of authentic conditions. But it depends upon how inflexible the human mentality has become or how fixedly identified we are with analysis and reason as the exclusive manner of human cognition. We will need to be considerably self-motivated in order to undertake the serious exploration of directly experienced reality because although self-perpetuating, immediate cognition requires scrupulously sincere application in order to be recognized as an authentic practice.

Knowledge through immediate cognition does not demand scholarship nor does it require peer evaluation in order to be justified. However, it is corroborated through direct experience because many experiential perspectives reveal the same elemental condition of essential existence.

Authenticity is recognized through the direct engagement of the human essence. There are no positions to argue because there is but one authentic dimension of existence and it is directly experienced through immediate engagement. The constructs of the intellectual elite become moot in the light of direct cognition. The intrinsic identity and authenticity of things are known experientially through an immediate encounter. They are recognized as vastly more significant than information derived through analysis and abstract rationalism concerning merely physical appearances. The myopic view of the determined materialist is recognized as obscure. Understanding, acquired obliquely through abstract rationalism, is similarly identified as of peripheral significance because the intrinsic existence of phenomena remains concealed to the indirect approach.

Through immediate cognition we definitively discover the significance of certain incorporeal phenomena. Our own, intrinsic identity itself is authenticated through immediate experience. It is recognized as real when it is experienced directly instead of attempting to adjudicate its existence through sequential reasoning and persuasive argument one way or another. The human, essential identity, as an incorporeal reality, remains incomprehensible and beyond the cognitive scope of conventional reasoning. It cannot be demonstrated as definitely extant by the intellect because it is materially elusive. But that does not mean that it has to be believed and accepted merely upon faith.

The human, conscious individuality is known to be definitively extant through immediate, self-recognition. We authenticate our essential existence through direct experience and recognizes our unique singularity. We experience ourselves as absolutely real and encounter our own original, intrinsic significance through immediate engagement.

It is evident through immanent experience that the essential and singular reality of others and the intrinsic identity of phenomena, share with us a dimension of incorporeal existence.

The three-fold nature of cognition outlined above, describes the dynamic consequence of immediate engagement, experienced similarly with respect to all phenomena. The human, intrinsic identity, without the influence of the intellect or of sentiment, engages an object immanently. It recognizes the reality of the existence of the essential phenomenon because it knows it immediately. The human essence does not have to reason the veracity of what it encounters because through the imminence of its approach it can only know reality. Further, it recognizes that phenomena possess intrinsic existence and discovers that their qualitative singularity is the essential identity.

Nothing separates the human, essential identity from an immediate experience of the intrinsic existence of phenomena. The human essence recognizes its own essential existence as its particular and singular distinction. Similarly, we look outward and recognize the same uniqueness, intrinsic identity and singular distinction, as the significant existence of every other person.

When the human quintessence gazes upon the world it discovers that it is populated with far more than merely physical appearances. It finds the inherent, qualitative distinctions between phenomena as their real identity. The merely superficial and blatantly obvious physiognomy, concluded to be exclusively authentic, is discovered to be the limited perspective of a materialistic, shallowness of observation. The human quintessence knows intrinsic identities for their essential authenticity, and it distinguishes phenomena by their qualitative distinctions, recognizing their authenticity through direct engagement.

The exclusively material perspective is one that is both restrictive and misleading. It implies that only the physical tangible has validity and that alarmingly, nothing else is real. The intellect supports this conjecture because it is unable to fathom the reality of something that is physically elusive. Cerebral thinking is inherently incapable of successfully dealing with intangibles and considers them non-evidence. Relying solely upon reason, the intellect will inevitably minimize the value of qualitative significances, challenging their very existence because they cannot be physically qualified. However, the human being experiences intangible realities such as qualities and values constantly. It follows that a discrepancy exists between intellectual assessment and knowledge through immediate experience. This is because the intellect most successfully manages only materially derived data while, conversely, immediate experience discerns the qualitative significance and the essential identity of phenomena.

Experiential cognition knows immediately of qualities and values and does not doubt their existence because it has engaged them from the perspective of the human, authentic identity. When the intellect and sentimental preference are sufficiently restrained in order that they may not interfere with experiential cognition, an entirely more meaningful reality than materialism becomes evident. The restraint of the intellect and of sentiment allows the human, essential identity to come to the fore. The human essence directly experiences the intrinsic, yet incorporeal identity of phenomena, as their authentic significance. The superficial appearance favored by the intellect pales in comparison. Indeed, the exclusivity of the material perspective is discovered to be a conspicuously narrow and misleading approach.

When conventional cognitive practices are restrained, we identify, through direct cognition, several significant fundamentals as definitively extant. We establish a certain caliber of intelligence founded upon immediate experience and steadily expand our knowledge of incorporeal realities. The reality of our own, singular existence is immediately experienced and known. Similarly, that of others may be also discerned. Further, we experience through an immediate encounter, without the assumption of prior understanding through association, that there exist identities, qualities and values as the root existence of physical appearances. We find that they are of vastly greater significance that the material semblance.

Further, we discover through immediate engagement and the concomitant intelligence that arises through the condition of our unique individuality, the existence of original organization that influences the material appearance. The ideal original is recognized as the established arrangements whereby, for example, organic phenomena organize. We know these to be works of great complexity because we recognize the manner whereby living forms move through metamorphic appearances in order to achieve a cycle of growth and development. Furthermore, we discern both conception and volition at work.

Obviously, the materialist cannot sanction the existence of purposeful, incorporeal organization, being convinced that the physical appearance is all there is in spite of an almost constant experience of intangible values to the contrary. Thus, the materialist denies personal, experiential knowledge and determinedly clings to an artificial construct that is ironically, merely, abstractly established. To the materialist, the direct cognition of intangible organization by the human, essential identity appears similar to belief and faith which is an anathema to the intellect that must be able to touch, measure and analyze something in order to establish its authenticity.

Belief and faith involve a trust that something may be valid even though it cannot be otherwise verified.

Direct cognition, whereby the unfettered, human, intrinsic identity and not the intellect, examines a phenomenon, is a superior, human, cognitive practice because it provides intelligence without having to obliquely analyze and evaluate appearances. But it is neither belief nor faith. The intellect cannot fathom this and, consequently, the materialist will proceed no further. Indeed, it is impossible to do so. Direct cognition requires the setting aside of abstract rationalism. The caliber of knowledge achieved through immediate experience cannot be intellectually deduced and evaluated but must be discovered through direct engagement by the human essence.

The hypothetical acceptance of something for the sake of argument, whose authenticity remains unproven, is a conventional, intellectual practice. An initial argument is established and further elaborated as if it were indeed real, in the hope that it may be verified through elaboration and qualified as authentic, through reason. Thus, those derided for their beliefs and faith by the materialist have, in fact, much in common with the accepted procedure of respectable research.

It is conceivable that the substance of something that is merely believed and faithfully trusted is, in fact, a reality. We may simply not have the means necessary to determine its authenticity. Paradoxically, an honest examination would reveal that human beings constantly deal with situations that must be accepted on trust and whose reality remains indemonstrable and unprovable.

This is the dilemma of every scrupulous inquiry whereby the existence of something is implied but can never be physically verified. However, the researcher, nonetheless, continues to explore further as if a postulate were real, using argument and logic in place of strict empiricism. But the existence of experientially authenticated, yet intangible organization, will always remain only hypothetical to conventional research because the indirect approach is incapable of demonstrating its authenticity.

The difficulty concerning a dimension of existence that is not physically represented is compounded when we attempt to justify and articulate intangible values, qualities and intrinsic identities. Yet, they are continually experienced by us in everyday life. It is undeniable that sunlight is far more consequential than is represented by abstract physics or by numerical symbolism. A few moments in the sunshine and we discover the intangible identity itself, through immediate experience. Our experiential knowledge is at odds with a string of numbers and equations that only represent those selected, physical attributes that are quantifiable. The exclusively materialistic approach avoids intrinsic identity and merely deals with the superficial properties of things.

Direct cognition is an inherent human faculty. There is nothing mysterious or mystical about it. It is merely that it is seldom practiced determinedly and purposefully because inevitably it requires the recognition

27

of the existence of the human, essential identity. Materialistic, Western philosophy does not recognize human incorporeality because it cannot demonstrate the authenticity of physically elusive phenomena. The materially exclusive mentality must, consequently discover a materially represented substitute.

The faculty through which direct cognition is achieved is exclusively intrinsic to the human, essential identity. But human identity is relegated to an inferior and derisive position in the face of the analytical scrutiny of the solely physical aspects of the human constitution. Appearances are considered substantial to the intellect because they are materially founded and, consequently, they are readily justified as authentic. Experientially known, yet intangible significances, by contrast, seem illusory. The rational materialist must, necessarily, also reject the incorporeal existence of human identity and replace it with something physical. The brain is that chosen organ.

Abstract conjecture founded upon the exhaustive analysis of material properties and the subsequent models and constructs established to represent them, cannot compete with experientially derived knowledge. The first is necessarily an indirect process of evaluation while direct cognition is an approach of immediate experience. They are incommensurable approaches to knowledge. The one deals exclusively with the ramifications of tangible evidence while the other immediately engages the qualitative distinctions that distinguish the intrinsic existence of phenomena.

Intangible qualities are dismissed by the conventional, materialistic approach because they are unfathomable to an intellect whose practice of cognition is established upon the abstract analysis of the tangible. Thus, the convinced materialist establishes a world-view founded exclusively upon physical properties. This unfortunate and stubborn conceit closes the way forward to further inquiry because it denies the existence of the most significant and essential, human cognitive-faculty whereby existence may be directly and experientially engaged.

Phenomena must be known experientially in order to be recognized implicitly. Yet, intelligence concerning qualitative distinctions and values, justified through direct cognition, is dismissed by conventional wisdom as ephemeral. An abstract, materially exclusive contrivance is established in the place of reality, in spite of what everyone experientially knows to the contrary concerning the authenticity of intangible significances.

Direct experience and knowledge derived through the attention of the human, essential identity recognizes that there are realities that can never be qualified through conventional reasoning. To be known they have to be immediately experienced. But it is not necessary to accept this upon belief or to faithfully adopt it. The human capacity of direct cognition and the adjunct faculty whereby we achieve existential intelligence concerning intangible realities through the authority of the human, essential identity, are inherent to the human constitution. They must, however, be personally explored and experienced in order to be justified.

The only way to authentically determine the intrinsic significance of a phenomenon is to engage it directly from the perspective of the human, essential identity. This has nothing to do with abstract rationalism and reasoned exposition. It is neither a preference nor a prejudice. It requires neither belief nor faith. It is entirely to do with a direct experience of the authentic condition of existence, through immediate engagement.

3. THE CONTRIVED NATURE OF MATERIALISM

The difficulty with materialism as an exclusive perspective towards existence is the inevitability of prejudice. Materialism excludes other approaches because it deals solely with tangible data. Its conclusions, therefore, will always be founded upon tangible evidence. Denying value to all physically unfounded information, it overreaches its jurisdiction and attempts to classify the entirety of existence upon an exclusively material basis.

This would be an acceptable approach if the materialist acknowledged that its researches can only span the tangible and that materialism was incapable of evaluating something of obvious intrinsic value that was without physical properties. But the exclusive philosophy of materialism is a human fallacy and an inappropriate extension of the scrutiny of material conditions inevitably leads to an excessively one-sided understanding. It is a perspective with inevitable and self-evident limitations because it exists within a certain frame of reference that possesses only relative importance. Extended beyond the province of the tangible aspects of existence it assumes that it is qualified to also determine the authenticity of intangible values. The materialist, convinced of the exclusive value of a physically limited approach denies the existence of anything intangible and thereby oversteps the bounds of its prerogative. It is inherently incapable of evaluating the existence of anything that is physically

31

unrepresented. By assuming that it is qualified it must inevitably suppose that the material appearances of phenomena are the entire basis of existence. Only interested in the physical aspect it endeavors to restrict the entirety of existence within those exclusive terms.

Materialistic, Western philosophy rejects the suggestion that genius resides in the workings of nature. This is sustained through the preconceived notion that if something cannot be physically demonstrated as extant, then how can it be known to really exist. It is further compounded by the insistence that all evidence concerning reality must be physically derived. This caution is commendable, empirical caution unless it results in closed-mindedness and an adamant prejudice against the impartial exploration of qualitative significances.

Yet, we would hope that even the staunchest materialist must concede significance through personal experience to at least some of the obvious, yet intangible phenomena. Unfortunately, a materialistic, philosophical construct has been established and accepted upon the authority of philosophical and scientific peer consensus. It sweepingly superimposes a contrived conviction to the detriment of experiential knowledge.

The materialist reasons abstractly, and theoretically, may confidently discard intangibles even in the face of universal familiarity. If personal experience of the existence of intangible authenticity seems to challenge the accepted, materialistic construct and appear beyond the grasp of abstract rationalism, it is discarded. Evidence is considered exclusively in the light of an affected outlook that while intimated experientially as untenable, yet remains steadfastly supported as valid. The contrived position is allowed to take precedence over knowledge derived from experience and it predictably winnows out that which does not readily conform to selectively materialistic preconditions. Thus, the materialist, through an abstract contrivance, successfully maintains an artificial interpretation of life founded exclusively upon physical evidence, even in the face of experiential contradiction.

While intangible realities are constantly experienced and known by us all, the contrived perspective declares that only physical properties are definitively justified. In practice however, even the most loyal advocate of materialistic, Western philosophy cannot avoid direct experience with the qualitative. Indeed, while they remain physically elusive, qualities are enormously significant to human experience.

The existence of physical properties is easy to qualify because they are blatantly recognizable, readily analyzed, and further, aspects of them may be quantified. Every detail can be labeled which gives the appearance of vast knowledge and profound authority. The appearance, however, is not the exclusive reality. Compared in significance to the qualitative distinction and the essential identity of a phenomenon, blatant appearances are regarded as superficial. The qualitative distinction is indicative of the singularity and inherent existence of a phenomenon. It is this that is the authentic identity of the object and not the merely physical attributes and properties. The intrinsic identity is experienced and recognized through immediate engagement to be of essential significance.

The recognition and justification of non-material realities through direct experience is a beginning step towards a wholesome knowledge concerning existence. If the imagination were allowed to wander and conceive of a world devoid of everything but physical properties, the resulting construct would be alien to life as we experience it. Very significant values including everything of a solely qualitative distinction would be missing. Qualities that are only experientially authenticated but universally acknowledged as significant, would be gone. In an exclusively physical and materialistically established landscape our sunshine for example, would be merely represented as a phenomenon of waves or particles with significance only to the mathematician and the physicist. We would lose the experientially known quality of sun warmth, the vitality of its influence upon all life and the ever-changing excitement of a natural color-scape. None of those qualities are successfully represented through their physical attributes alone. Their intrinsic existence must be experientially determined.

The exclusively materialistic position is, therefore recognized as an abstract, intellectual invention that contradicts immediate experience and, through its selectivity, it is recognized as a condition alien to reality. The significance of the qualitative dimension to existence cannot be excluded. But materialism does not know what to do with it, and therefore, excludes the qualitative dimension from serious consideration. The result is a one-sided philosophy that emphasizes the physical appearances of things. Exclusive materialism, as a transparent construct of our imagination, is the conceptual consequence of an abstract position that is pursued to its logical, although ridiculous, conclusion. Upon closer examination it is even logically unsustainable, but ironically, it continues to be a position stubbornly maintained through conviction alone.

Challenged by knowledge obtained through an immediate experience of qualitative distinctions and significances that are otherwise intangible, we discover that the flaw of materialistically founded philosophy lies in its exclusivity. Qualities of only a certain caliber are permitted while anything that portends and alludes to the existence of a universal, incorporeal existence is dashed aside. This prejudice is the consequence of an abhorrence of anything that smacks of so-called spirituality.

The immanent condition of incorporeal significances is misunderstood and maligned as if it were an unfounded belief. If we were to imagine, as we did before, a world now composed of those qualitative distinctions and intrinsic identities, in the manner whereby we described the quality of the sunshine, what a rich and vibrant depiction that would be and a complete contrast to the materialistic scenario. This is in fact, the reality of the incorporeal dimension and we already dwell in the midst of it. We have merely replaced reality with a barren counterfeit. Physical appearances and properties only tangentially represent the qualitative dimension that is recognized, through immediate experience, as the immanent condition of existence.

The open-minded observer cannot possibly discount intangible qualities. To do so would be paramount to insanity. We would be denying all that we experientially know to be essential for a contrived conviction that insists that only superficial appearances warrant attention. Therefore, impartially, we recognize the restrictive nature of humanly fabricated systems and structures and we are determined to know things originally, for ourselves. We desire to know reality and we are impatient with contrived and slanted explanations that insist upon a perspective at odds with our own experience. The unbiased researcher includes phenomena of every description without preference or selectivity, even if they exist intangibly. Nothing is summarily dismissed in order to conform with an established, pre-conceptual structure.

As explored above, materialism is fueled by a prejudice. It is imagined that if value is ceded to experientially authenticated, intangible qualities and inherent identities through direct cognition, then unsubstantiated beliefs of every caliber are also included. This demonstrates both a lack of knowledge concerning the dynamic of direct cognition and a complete ignorance of the incorporeal dimension of existence. The immediate engagement of a phenomenon does not permit fiction. It is a direct experience of singular identities and qualitative distinctions by the discerning, human quintessence. It reveals the identity of something founded upon its particular quality, value and intrinsic existence. Phenomena are not interpreted based upon their material appearances nor abstractly determined. They are identified by the quality of their intrinsic distinction.

The materialist is afraid that the opposite approach to an abstractly reasoned world-view, composed exclusively of physical properties, would be unsubstantiated belief and superstition. This is far from the case. Direct cognition requires as much discipline as empiricism and will not allow fantasy to insinuate itself as knowledge. The inclusion of experientially derived knowledge of the intangible dimension of existence compounds and qualifies the physical, revealing things as they are in reality, and not as they are otherwise, abstractly reasoned to be. The physical appearance is recognized as a merely superficial perspective and it is not mistaken for the intrinsic identity of the phenomenon.

The contrived notion that the world consists merely of tangible attributes only makes sense abstractly. The weakness of this theoretical position lies in the selective nature of the information that forms its basis. Materialism is an artificial construct founded upon partial and incomplete data extracted solely from physical appearances. It remains a remote concept even from the personal experience of the individual who maintains its authenticity. A world void of intangible qualities, identities and essentials is a grim prospect indeed but the materialist insists that it is justified. Materialism is a surmised perspective, indirectly reasoned from one category of information. The peripheral approach of the materialist requires an emphatic denial of all qualities, that while intangible, remain directly known to every human being through experience. Materialism cannot be both selective and consistent, even though the denial of some self-evident intangibles is patently absurd.

The missing dimension of the exclusively, materialistic world-view is the qualitative, essential significance of phenomena. It consists of the intrinsic identities that belie appearances. Its deficiency makes materialism a contrived perspective because contrary to the construct that maintains the opposite, qualities possess significant existence that is profoundly authentic and experientially recognizable to everyone.

The significant reality of obvious qualitative values known universally, is indicative of a dimension of existence, that while physically insubstantial, remains experientially authenticated as extant.

Through abstract reasoning, established solely upon information regarding the peripheral attributes of phenomena, a model is established that bears no resemblance to experiential reality. Through logical, sequential argument conclusions are maintained that clearly contradict experience. They may be established as true through systematic rationalism, yet they remain remote from reality. They are demonstrated as unreal through normal, human familiarity with the qualitative values of existence. This should be a severe warning to those who exclusively credit the abstract reasoning faculties while simultaneously ignoring knowledge obtained through an immediate encounter. Abstract assessment is bound to be ambiguous as a cursory indulgence of exclusive materialism immediately demonstrates. The obscurity of the materialistic perspective is immediately revealed and recognized as erroneous when compared to intelligence through experiential cognition. This is because experiential engagement reveals the essential existence of phenomena that is not otherwise, physically apparent.

Unfortunately, the materialistic contrivance does considerable harm to the disposition of those who embrace it. It is itself a belief system similar to any other by virtue of its theoretical status and the indirectness of its fabrication. It is a calculated and depressing perspective towards life, spawned abstractly and maintained stubbornly in the face of experientially engaged reality.

Direct experience makes a mockery of the narrow perspective of materialism because it recognizes the much fuller and more significant extent of reality. It reveals the limitation of the intellect as the sole adjudicator for determining that which is authentic because experience demonstrates that qualitative significance, as an extant dimension of existence, is missing from abstract rationalization.

The intrinsic distinction between phenomena is known through direct experience by the quality, value and significance of their existence. While they are all intangible, these meaningful essentials cannot be omitted from a comprehensive evaluation. Otherwise, it would be as if one were to establish a language without adjectives, adverbs or figurative speech, void of dimensionality.

Abstract, deductive evaluation, called upon to qualify a materialistic, linear definition of life through argument and sequential reasoning, only exacerbates an already absurd perspective. Reasoning is recognized as limited by virtue of its distance from the phenomena. It tries to calculate what something is because that is what it does most efficiently. But qualitative significances cannot be adequately quantified and represented in their entirety for reason to successfully evaluate. Qualitative distinctions are conspicuous only to immediate experience and recognized for the authenticity of their existence through direct encounter. Indirect evaluation can offer little further elucidation.

The logical extension of an exclusively materialistic perspective presents only a shallow evaluation of existence. No phenomenon is limited merely to its physical properties, yet the materialist insists otherwise. The extrapolated position of materialism reveals a world-view at odds with our own experience, but we accept it because it is logically and authoritatively presented, and we accordingly doubt the value of first-hand, experiential intelligence.

The materialistic, Western philosophical view is a sterile appraisal lacking all dimension and qualitative value. It is a contrived and alien product of an abstract mentality. The materialist prefers the abstract construct over direct experience because the intellect is of such a nature that it manages information concerning physical properties very convincingly. The argumentatively represented, materialistic position is logically compelling because it draws from tangibly established information. It can quantify and calculate those aspects of phenomena that can be numerically represented and claim that the physical appearance is the extent of reality. It can order physical properties systematically because they are tangible and it can analyze something that is material and reduce it into component parts.

But qualitative distinctions cannot be analyzed. The mistake is in imagining that the tangible aspects and functions of phenomena, which the intellect manages very well, are the full extent of existence. The intellect falls short when it attempts to evaluate values because the cerebral organ is physical and deals most favorably with its common nature. Yet, the physicality of phenomena is only of peripheral significance. Fortunately, the human being has an alternative faculty of cognition for intangibles. Essential significances are engaged, authenticated and justified through immediate apprehension by the human, essential identity.

There is no such thing as a comprehensive, philosophical approach towards life. Existence, including ourselves must be known directly, in its entirety. An intellectual artifice established as a means of interpreting and understanding life will inevitably neglect some elements by virtue of its indirect nature. Materialism neglects intangibles. But qualities cannot not be dismissed merely because they have no material basis. Otherwise, we establish an interpretation of existence upon only selective evidence. The intellect may not be able to abstractly manage intangibles, but it does not follow that qualities, values and intrinsic identities are nonexistent. Attempting to dismiss everything that cannot be physically demonstrated suggests a determined, philosophical myopia that serves no one. The intellect is inappropriate when it comes to identifying something essentially. Even though an abstractly reasoned interpretation of life may at first, appear formidable, it is recognized through comparison with direct cognition, as conceit and not genius, when the result is a contrived structure remote from experientially known reality.

By banishing qualities, values and intangible, intrinsic identities from an evaluation of life and declaring them negligible, the materialist rejects the perspective of a significant cognitive faculty of the human constitution. Furthermore, the profound, individual significance of the human being is similarly discarded because the authenticity our singular existence rests upon our intrinsic distinction and not upon our appearance.

An exclusively materialistic philosophy is an extreme, abstract distortion. It is as if the value of touch were alone elevated above all the other faculties of sense and one remained doggedly determine to describe all life upon that basis alone. It is impossible to know what something is definitively, solely upon an examination of the physical properties. Accomplished, is an exclusively physical perspective described in endlessly minuscule detail. Physical appearances without the inclusion of qualities and values offer only a very meager representation of reality. The consequence of an exclusively materialistic perspective towards life is a world-view that is counterfeit, wherein only the physical, mechanical and mathematical properties are adequately represented and the mere superficial is ceded exclusive reality. It is an abstract contrivance and an emaciated substitute for reality.

The missing dimension from the materialistic, philosophical approach towards life is retrieved through the immediate engagement of phenomena by the human, essential identity. Experiential cognition is the direct approach that does not require evaluation and abstract rationalism.

Direct, experiential cognition consists of two aspects. The first is the immediate experience of the phenomenon whereby the actuality of its existence is recognized through immanent engagement. Alone, this experience is a significant barometer and standard against which a contrived definition of reality can be compared. The real is directly encountered and experientially known. Artificial, abstract systems and contrivances are revealed as deficient. Similarly, that which is merely hypothetical or imaginatively conceived is readily recognized as an oblique and obscure construction.

The second aspect of the direct approach is the intelligence that arises when a phenomenon is encountered in present time, with an open mind, as if it were the first occasion upon which it was being experienced. The knowledge that arises concerning the object of interest is forthcoming when the authentic and intrinsic identity of the human being confronts something directly. It is through these two facets of cognition that the essential nature and qualitative distinctions of phenomena are discerned.

The direct, experiential engagement of phenomena is a human, cognitive necessity because it reveals the authentic condition of existence. Through abstraction rationalism and sentiment, we dwell in a mentality that is remote from reality. Reality is an unknown condition to either of these approaches. Occasionally, during our everyday lives, we may suddenly encounter the authentic existence as if by caprice. The immediacy of the experience takes our breath away. Through some auspicious condition the human, intrinsic authority comes to the fore and we encounter reality immediately. But experiences of this kind need not occur merely through chance. Instead of an occasional and fortuitous happenstance, reality may be directly experienced as a natural condition through the acknowledgment and immediate engagement of the human, essential identity.

These capricious events of experiential cognition occur when the intellect is still and phenomenal evaluation, through sentimental preference, is caught off-guard. The human essential immediately engages a circumstance, and it is experienced in its extant condition. The otherwise neglected, qualitative dimension is directly and experientially authenticated, and the fullness of existence is recognized.

It is this universally acknowledged, capricious experience that convinces us of a far more expansive reality than that which we conventionally imagine. This is precisely the reality that is accessible to every human being through immediate experience by the essential distinction of our constitution. The remembrance of the vivid expansiveness and thrill of the experience will spur our enthusiasm to eagerly explore the condition of immediate engagement in order that it may become a consistent perspective and not merely an extraordinary anomaly. Furthermore, the sadness that results from the fleeting rarity of the experience provide additional incentive towards further research.

The human, essential nature itself is directly recognized as authentic when it is experienced through an immediate event of cognition. The same manner whereby we encounter the fullness of reality is applied to our own existence. The human quintessence is an intrinsic singularity whose existence is intellectually indeterminable because to understand it would stretch the capacity of reason beyond its prerogative. The existence of an intangible thing may be qualified or denied through reason but it can never be definitely known by abstract evaluation.

It is ironic that the reasoned constructs that are pursued by the materialist, promoted with conviction and presented as if they were real, are revealed as merely, educated belief in the light of direct cognition.

The human, essential existence recognizes its own authenticity and that of others. It also has the capacity to discover alike, incorporeal qualities, similar in nature to itself, as the significance of phenomenal appearances. Cognition of this nature is made possible by the authentic, human identity that is known to be real through experiential knowledge. The human, conscious individuality recognizes its own existence and through immediate cognition engages the full magnitude of reality.

4. ORIGINAL PRINCIPLE

The immediate engagement of natural circumstances reveals the original significance of things and puts one's own self in proper perspective. We might otherwise imagine that our discoveries of physical law or the properties and activities of nature, entitle us to take credit and assume mastery.

Our existence is remarkable, and the realization of our particular individuality is an astonishingly significant experience, but we are not of our own invention. The existence and workings of nature are not of human achievement. We discover a cellular structure, photosynthesis or discern the systematic nature of inheritance but cannot assume that because something appears to be explained that it is also of our inauguration.

Immediate engagement reveals a significant dimension to existence that establishes an entirely different perspective towards both nature and the human being. It becomes shameful to us to assume a self-conceited position towards anything as we recognize that our discoveries are less to our own credit, but rather present an ever-increasing perception of the grandeur and majesty of existence.

We deserve merit for our diligence but none for the substance of our discoveries because we receive our reward through the expansion of our perspective towards the immensity and richness of existence. The most appropriate attitude towards our miraculous existence and that of nature is modesty. It is a suitable and unpretentious stance to assume towards something that is none of our own making.

Through direct engagement, the human, intrinsic identity discerns the genius of an original ideal according to which all organic life is organized. It recognizes the activity of a virtuoso in the establishment of the metamorphic intricacies and the transformative dynamics of organisms. Complex, functioning relationships involving precisely appropriate components are organized immaculately towards very specific ends. All living form diversity corresponds to general systems of organic functioning that are structured in an intrinsically similar fashion. The manner whereby an organism will metamorphose through different appearances, while remaining qualitatively consistent in its identity, demonstrates an astonishing conceptual intricacy.

This insight is less challenging when it is compared to the experience whereby we recognize the hand of the artisan at work in a fabricated article. We examine a humanly, manufactured item and readily determine that someone conceived of the object, applied volition towards its realization and manufactured it purposefully, selecting particular materials to do so. Further, we recognize upon closer scrutiny, that conceptualization, volition and realization are universally essential to all human production. We discern this through a direct, open-minded examination of the completed item.

In nature the process is similarly in evidence. The inauguration of a metamorphic dynamic, whereby a living cycle of activity is established, and different phases of development and appearance conspire to achieve the goal of organic, reproducing life, is clearly the consequence of genius and volition, not mere caprice. Those who have failed to observe and recognize the compound intricacies of nature through immediate engagement, and have only analyzed the superficial, physical properties, will not discover anything beyond mechanics. They will fail to determine that, purposeful intent and methodology are quite evident and readily recognizable, from the repeated incidences of metamorphic reinterpretation that occur in accordance with the overall necessity of the organic composition.

The term growth, when applied to organisms, is a misnomer if it is understood to mean merely an increase in proportion. Expansion in nature is accomplished stage by stage through crucial transformational leaps. The same essential identity is transformed constantly, metamorphosing into diverse expressions towards the realization of a particular conceptual organization.

The estranged perspective and peculiar position that insists upon capricious originality and accidental creativity arises through our habitually abstract manner of considering phenomena. We ponder situations remotely and try to understand them in terms of what we already know, instead of engaging them immediately.

In order to discover the original condition of a thing, we must set aside preconceived interpretations and associations and engage the object originally. Otherwise, we merely rearrange prior intelligence but fail to recognize the extant condition of the phenomenon as it exists essentially.

When the human, essential identity directly engages any phenomenon, the event will be discovered in its authentic condition of existence. The phenomenon of a plant reveals a consistency of activity that is recognized as common to all flora. We discover through immediate attention, the invariable procedure of a metaphoric transformation that exists as an unending cycle. Sequentially, transformation culminates in the achievement of an event of fulfillment and the apogee of leaf, flower, or a bud is accomplished as an inevitable and consistent occurrence. The metamorphic cycle does not commence at any particular stage but transformative appearance and reappearance through one culmination or another may be recognized at any juncture. It becomes readily apparent that organisms follow a commonality of arrangement in spite of their differences in appearance. Two plants may differ enormously, both qualitatively and in consequent appearance, but they share the essential and consistent commonalities of a metamorphic transformation. That which is recognized as essentially common to all plants, irrespective of their particular appearance, is indicative of the archetypal plant concept. The floral concept exists intrinsically, while the particular plant variation remains qualitatively distinct.

We recognize conceptualization, volition and realization at work when we directly observe the phenomenon of form metamorphosis. Organic life metamorphoses purposely towards the accomplishment a certain result. The conceptual structure, that is relentlessly pursued by all flora, is recognized as an establishment of metamorphic transformations towards the culmination of specific events. The existence of a cyclical, metamorphic structure as the consistent necessity of all plant life provides evidence of the existence of a will to establish its formulation and its subsequent application.

The commonality of development that is consistence to all organic life possesses a similarity of structure, yet there is also a clear distinction between a plant or animal archetype. They are alike essentially in the manner of their composition as metamorphic procedures and events, but differ decidedly when adapted to different organic circumstances.

If, in our imagination, we were to remove the appearance of the organic phenomenon from the plant or animal and engage solely the conceptual organization, we would encounter the archetype. An exploration of the plant or animal concept in this original condition reveals both the archetypal intricacy and the genius of its establishment. We do not conventionally recognize this because through reduction and analysis we diminish the extraordinary magnitude of organic existence and suppose it to be elementary.

Of necessity, we apply conceptualization, volition and realization to all human manufacture. Yet, nature is denied that courtesy. But, if we are creative, and furthermore, the offspring of nature, then nature must also intrinsically possess that same capacity and competence, otherwise we could not be endowed with it ourselves. While no one seriously challenges the integration of the human being within a vast and complex natural ecology, yet materialistic, Western philosophy denies conceptualization to nature and attributes the existence and diversity of organisms to capricious, physical forces. The weakness of this materialistic position is revealed as self-evident through simple reasoning.

Through direct cognition, one engages phenomena inclusively of one's own self and not merely as a remote spectator who dispassionately observes, as if the situation were of no personal consequence. Things are experienced directly and immediately, and recognized for their intrinsic identity through the aegis of our own intrinsic singularity of existence. Existence is vastly more significant than can be determined by the remote onlooker because the objective viewer does not engage phenomena from the perspective of the human, essential existence but endeavors to maintain a distance. But the involvement of the observer is vital to immediate experience. The imminence of a direct encounter through our own significance, allows us to experience things as they are in reality, not merely as they seem from a peripheral point of view. The objective observer cannot discover the authentic condition of existence because it requires experiential engagement to do so. Subjective experience through the human, essential identity is a vital dynamic of immediate cognition.

While subjectivity is necessary for direct cognition, it should not be misconstrued as if immediate engagement were merely a form of sentimental preference or conceptual prejudice. Subjectivity, in this case, means that the human, incorporeal existence engages the phenomenon immediately. But things are not evaluated from the perspective of the feeling-sentient or corporeal nature. The irony is that subjectivity through the aegis of the human, incorporeal existence reveals the definitive identity of phenomena, while conventional objectivity is recognized as an inadequate perspective because it does not directly engage. It cannot offer conclusive evidence because the abstract evaluation of physical appearances is incapable of achieving irrefutable, intrinsic identification. The human, incorporeal existence, however, remains intransient. It is of far greater consequence than conventionally understood objectivity because being itself of absolute existence, it only recognizes the similarly, real condition of other phenomena.

Abstract thinking that manages ideas, is necessarily superseded by direct cognition involving experience. The first is apparently objective but, in reality, merely remote. The latter involves the human, essential identity. The human, intrinsic singularity is personally experienced and from its perspective a phenomenon is immediately engaged. The individual directly recognizes its own authenticity and is similarly, struck with astonishment at the authentic existence of other phenomena. Formerly the object was only known obliquely. Now, the human, essential identity, in present timing, encounters something directly and knows it straightforwardly, unsullied by preconceptions and sentiment.

Immediate, experiential cognition reveals the tenor and quality of essential existence. We discover what reality is like through the immediate engagement of the human essence with an object, because we experience phenomena directly, through our own essential identity. Reality is an experientially known condition that cannot be surmised or conjectured. It is quite independent of what we might imagine it to be and entirely contradicts our abstractly formulated conjectures because it is indeterminable through reason.

The manner whereby the conventional, abstract reduction of nature may be tried and evaluated for its authenticity, requires a qualitative comparison with something that is known to be absolutely real. In this case we select something that is materially represented by its effect, while simultaneously remaining nonphysical. It is something that is identified intrinsically as extant through direct cognition and also further qualified through reasonable argument.

We engage a situation immediately and observe, for example, two varieties within the same genus such as the oak-tree and recognize that they both adhere to the same oak-tree principle. Musically, they may be described as variations upon the same Quercus theme. Further, we expand our considerations and observe different varieties of any tree and recognize that they all, similarly, conform to an underlying, general complex of principles. This conformity qualifies them all as trees.

We discover that variations are different ways in which the same general arrangement and organization is expressed. However, it should not be assumed with increasing familiarity, that the principles that comprise a tree are simple. Through recognition of the variations in manner in which the same principle is specifically expressed, we err considerably if we imagine that the structure of organic organization is elementary, or if we think that we know all about the archetype. In fact, the archetype is less a musical score and may be more appropriately described as an entire symphonic organization.

5. ARCHETYPAL CONCEPTION

The general principle, according to which all trees must comply in order to be considered trees may be named the ideal, tree conception. Classically, the ideally established, dynamical structure, according to which all variations of the same foundational compound of principles corresponded, was termed the archetype. Thus, through direct cognition we recognize the reality of something intangible, that is also both complex and purposeful. The archetype is qualified as authentic through an immediate encounter with the phenomenon by the human, essential identity. The contrived, abstract interpretation of nature appears very meager in comparison to a complexity of arrangement of such working intricacy and significance. Capricious, natural organization is an unsightly contradiction, acceptable to no one, unless they are approach nature from a condition of determined prejudice.

Increasingly, we become familiar with the nature of the ideal commonality or archetype, and determine its authenticity through physical evidence. It is progressively recognized as a vastly intricate mandate of organization and metamorphic transformation, while simultaneously remaining intangibly existent. We recognize it as authentic through its resolute constancy even when we see it revealed through a multitude of different appearances. Our observations demonstrate the existence of a compound order of immense complexity and coherence. This perception establishes an experiential foundation of knowledge concerning the nature of reality. We come to know something as definitively real, that at the same time exists only incorporeally. Against this caliber of intelligence, abstractly conceived postulations concerning existence, may be successfully tried for their authenticity.

We recognize the quality of the existent, yet intangible, ideal precedent of the tree and thereby we determine, through qualitative comparison, whether theoretical contentions and beliefs concerning existence, ring true, or fail to compare. Through immediacy, we become familiar with the qualitative and intrinsic nature of reality and wary of the hypothetical construct that proposes an alternative interpretation that is exclusively, physically founded.

The archetype is something that cannot be provoked into being either by physical forces, natural law or through an evolutionary process because it is a complex organization that can only be conceived. It cannot be established through uncreative influences. Further, it must be consistently entire and immaculate in order to function. It could never be half-evolved. It is indicative of an ignorance of reality, and of a preoccupation with abstract conceptualization, that suggests that the concept of organic organization arose capriciously or in a piece-meal fashion. There is no such

60

thing as a partly working organism and there never was. If the archetype is incompletely applied then, it fails to function and if a life-form fails to conform entirely to the principles of the archetype, it will miscarry.

Yet, the conceptual composition that is the archetype, cannot be physically realized if the Agencies of life are absent. Air, water, warmth and sunlight must exist and must similarly, always have existed in tandem with the archetype, for organisms to have a physical existence. The archetype can exist alone, conceptually, without the Agencies of life but an organism can never be physically realized unless the archetype, the Agencies and biomaterial are all simultaneously apparent.

Similarly, the activity whereby nutrients are taken and transmuted according to the requirements of the organism is also a metamorphic dynamic of a most intriguing kind. Not only does it reveal chemical and biochemical transmutation as metamorphic in nature, it also offers a glimpse into the intricacy of the structure of archetypal conceptualization itself and its ingenious performance.

Flora can metamorphose minerals into biochemicals through the influence of the Agencies that vivify the plant and the archetypal intricacy of the organism. But the organism must be extant in order to thrive and nothing happens by virtue of the Agencies alone. This implies that the organism, including its archetypal organization and the Agencies must always have been coexistent throughout the entire history of life upon Earth.

Individually, different varieties of the same organism reveal the ideal precedent according to their own nature of implementation. But they must all conform in principle to the established structure of the archetype in order to remain viable.

Analysis and scrutiny of organisms in order to discover their workings reveals more of the intricacies of the archetype. But the entirety is not defined by its processes. While the archetype is the general conceptualization of myriad organic varieties, it is nonetheless, always a unified entirety. The character of expression reveals the nature of the plant or creature but the archetype remains an immaculate, unified body of interwoven strategy.

The archetype is not a simple thing. It is the entire living organization of the organism at every moment of activity throughout its cycle. Inherent within the ideal system is the compound complexity whereby the archetypal structure carries the living substance through different stages of achievement in order to attain a preordained cycle of development. It reinvents and refashions the organic entirety, in order to advance a particular necessity, through an unfolding sequence of events. The archetype convolutes and remakes the organism consecutively according to the requirement of each momentary event within the cycle of growth. This is the intricacy whereby a cycle of living activity takes place. The dynamic of the archetype reestablishes living substance differently according to the need of every momentary position within its overall composition. Further, through the recognition of established, sequential arrangement and organization towards the achievement of a living cycle, one recognizes the inherency of purposefulness.

Yet, the archetype is only corporeally in evidence through its organizational mandate. Left to itself, the archetype propels its formless way through various progressions and convolutions as a flawless formulation. The unspecified archetype is recognized as a conceptual arrangement. It appears physically only in the context of an organism. All organic variations possess a similar archetypal organization although they appear different according to the manner of their expression. The qualitative difference that distinguishes different variations resides not with the archetype but is recognized as the distinct identity of the particular organism.

The archetype uses the dynamic of metamorphic transformations in order to establish the organizational principles of a living composition. It reasserts its directive continuously, even in the case of injury. Healing is a further vindication of the existence of the archetype. Meanwhile, the distinct identity of the creature is best artistically and qualitatively described as the motif whereby the common ideal is particularized.

The motif does not clash with the archetype, but the particular distinction of the organism must comply with the archetypal mandate. A plant such as an onion is qualitatively distinct. Yet, it obeys the archetypal definition of a plant. The bulb is not an abnormal root but a truncated stem that consists of a concentration of leaves. The hollow stalk that later rises to star-burst of flowers at the tips of long shoots, similarly reveals a consistency of motif.

In every moment, the identical, essential motifs of expression that distinguishes an organism, is expressed comprehensively throughout the entirety. Regardless of the location within the composition, the same motif is consistently represented and remains true to the intrinsic nature of the organism throughout the entire, metamorphic cycle. This is the reason why the DNA of every cell of a living organization is found to be identical. DNA is the physical representation of the motif. The motif is consistently revealed as the qualitative expression of the organism throughout all alternative, metamorphic expressions, and in every particular. But it should not be confused with the archetype. The archetype itself is the undifferentiated working-concept of the entirety. The archetype is the conceptual organism, while the motif is the manner whereby the organism is particularly distinguished.

Metamorphic transformation, according to the

requirements of function and the position within the living whole, reveals the dynamic nature whereby the archetypal composition is established. That compound conceptualization which arranges the entire composition of living, metamorphosing appearances in order to achieve a life cycle, remains ideal and intangible because it is the conceptual entirety itself. It is not represented except as the functioning wholeness of an organism. It is only physically revealed through the metamorphic dynamics and functions of living organisms. The completeness, including the entire, dynamical complexity of operation according to purpose and intention, is the archetype, while the distinction of the organism is represented as the particular a motif of expression. The archetype can be determined through direct cognition as the ideal arrangement, recognized as the commonalities of dynamic organization, consistent to all variations. Two plants differ distinctly in appearance, yet possesses commonalities that identify them as plants. That which identifies plant life as such, is the archetype. The archetype is always present as the functioning entirety, yet it remains illusive in appearance because of the physical prominence of the particular motif whereby the organism is expressed.

An organism is always complete at every moment of appearance be it as seed or in maturity. The leaf is entirely the same essentially and qualitatively as the stem. We observe the seed or the mature form and imagine that the one represents the entirety more significantly than the other. Both appearances are the complete organism in different metamorphic guises. The particular appearance at any moment is the manner whereby the singularity of expression is revealed according to the requirements and demands of the archetype. The archetype consists of the dynamic integrality of the organism. The familiar organism is the archetype represented in a particular manner. Imagined uninterpreted and unexpressed according to a particular motif, the archetype is recognized as it is in actuality. It is a raw, conceptual synthesis. It is the compound original of the life-form including all of its functioning and operation.

To suggest that the archetype is non-existent because it remains ideal is a considerable error and one typical of abstract thinking. The archetype exists as the impeccable wholeness of the organism. The entirety of every organic expression is a realized archetype. It is an utterly authentic and a far more significant than the transitory, physical appearance because it exists essentially. It remains intangible and is only physically represented through the dynamic processes of the living organism.

Through quiet observation we recognize both genius, volition and realization at work in the intricacies of the archetype as well as in the miraculous reality of life itself through the aegis of the Agencies. Yet, without the existence of the archetype, expressed as the overall organic concept, the organism remains merely, undefined biomaterial. The archetype is recognized as without physical substance but lacking its presence, there would be no organic organization.

Similarly, the metamorphic cycle of the butterfly reveals the consistency of the motif of its expression. The particular butterfly distinction is always fully represented whether as the egg, the caterpillar, the chrysalis or the winged insect. The form appearances differ according to the demands of the insect archetype, yet they remain qualitatively identical and consistently complete. If the egg were somehow something juvenile and wanting, it could not metamorphose as an immaculate butterfly. If at any moment between the stages of the chrysalis and butterfly, the creature were incompletely represented, metamorphic reformation would be impossible. However, an organic form may appear at any time it will always remain entire even if represented by a single egg or examined between different stages of culmination. The motif remains consistence as does the constant condition of metamorphoses.

In addition, there is another layer of complexity established within the ideal original or archetype. The cycle of a perpetual transformation embraces the possibility of continued variation whereby the particular interpretation or variety of expression may be adjusted and refined according to the restraints and demands of the compound ecology that influences the physical circumstances of the organism. These variations are introduced into the motif during reproduction. Ecological duress requires an adjustment to the particular manner whereby the ideal original is interpreted. In animals, changes occur in the temper or demeanor of the creature because the animal is almost exclusively feeling sentient. The distinct identity or motif of expression alters according to the change in essential character. In the vegetable and arthropod kingdoms, the pressure of the ecology changes the nature of the plant or insect directly.

These alterations in expression are limited, in our time, to the scope and range of the particular, accumulated distinction of the creature. Through the entrenchment of specialization, the form becomes progressively defined and consequently limited in its capacity to change. The demeanor of the creature may still alter, but typically an animal will adjust only behaviorally because the possibility of form change has become extremely restricted through the narrowing of options by increased definition. A general, undefined form may originally have changed dramatically in demeanor and consequent form gesture yet, the possibility of the entirety of a specific form, dynamically reinterpreting itself according to a reversal of demeanor, becomes increasingly restricted through the accumulated parameters of form distinction. A creature's potential for change is restricted to the particular condition in which it currently exists. Thus, animals in our time, that cannot successfully adapt to extreme ecological challenge behaviorally, will become extinct.

The rat will prosper in a wide variety of contexts while the giraffe perishes quickly if separated from its optimum environment. The rat can readily survive through a slight behavioral adjustment while the giraffe must fundamentally change in structure in order to adapt to an aquatic, arboreal or subterranean context. Form adaption for the giraffe is virtually unimaginable because it is highly specialized. The rat, however, does not have to change in temperament in order to survive, it merely adjusts its behavior.

Recognition of the intangible dimension of existence may be expanded beyond a general appreciation of the organic archetype. As mentioned earlier, an intimacy exists between viable, organic organization, established according to the ideal precedent and life itself. Life must always be coexistent with the organism and both must always have existed simultaneously. The Agencies that an organic organization must have, include air, water, warmth and sunlight. Without their presence life fails. Therefore, inherent within the Agencies are qualities that sustain life. They remain elusive, yet they are of greater significance to nature than the merely, physically recognized properties. While physically indiscernible, the incorporeal qualities that sustain life are evident through immediate experience. All four maintain life collectively, yet each is of a distinctly different caliber. Organic life requires all four continuously.

Any disparity or discrepancy of impact between the agencies must be included within the complex of ecological influences that act upon the creature or plant. As such, the unevenness of distribution between air, water, warmth and sunlight as ecological factors, is influential upon the organic condition and serves as a catalyst of form change.

The archetype exists as an arrangement and organization of metamorphosing relationships established to achieve a cycle of growth and development. Established within the dynamical structure of the archetype is the manner whereby the influences of the agencies are ideally utilized. Without the Agencies of life organic forms can never be physically realized. Similarly, without the archetype there is no organization and, therefore, there remains nothing to animate. It is readily evident that the Agencies of life and the ideal conception of immaculate, organic organization, exist in perpetual correspondence or each would otherwise remain impotent and moot.

Thus, another glimpse is possible through direct cognition and simple reasoning whereby a deeper appreciation for the complex nature of the archetype is achieved. The orchestration of living organization takes all factors into consideration. Recognition of the enormous intricacy of the archetype is further evidence of its reality. Simplification, through abstract conceptualization, merely reduces the ideal in significance and the authenticity of its existence becomes increasingly elusive. The difference in value between direct, experiential cognition and oblique abstraction is starkly revealed. The former is an immediate experience of how things are in actuality while the other attempts evaluation through rationalism.

Direct cognition is a practice that involves immediate engagement whereby the essential existence of a phenomenon is determined through straightforward experience. The human, essential identity discovers not only the authenticity of its own existence but also the intrinsic identity of others and the significances that belie phenomenal appearances. Animals cannot do the same. They dwell in a heightened feeling and instinctual consciousness. Their identity is realized by the group, the herd or flock. Only the human being has a singularity of identity. The realization and direct experience of the human, essential identity and the recognition of the intrinsic significance of phenomena provides a qualitative benchmark of reality against which philosophies and beliefs may be compared for their legitimacy.

Familiarity and the recognition of the tenor of incorporeal reality, it is further augmented and compounded by the subjective involvement of the intrinsic nature of the human being. It thereby becomes evident that we are not aloof from nature and that the human body is also composed according to an archetypal ideal just like everything else. The human body did not somehow self-construct but is conceived of a source beyond itself to serve our essential existence. It is thoroughly justified to acknowledge the Earthly context of the human body and the incorporeal nature of its inception but immediate experience through the human, essential existence, also reveals that the ipseity is of incorporeal significance.

If that were not sufficient to secure a profound appreciation of what incorporeal existence is like, direct cognition further impacts the silent attention of the observer with wonder concerning the realization that these things indeed exist and are thoroughly real. This gives rise to an astonishment that is unachievable through an examination of the simplistic constructs and contrived systems that we abstractly establish in order to explain away the world in materialistic terms. Direct cognition gives rise to amazement because formally we only evaluated something abstractly and indirectly. It is indeed extraordinary to engage something immediately from the perspective of the unfettered human, essential identity and experience it as it exists in reality.

Armed with this experiential and reasonable knowledge of the incorporeal we may appraise and compare all declarations and testimonies concerning the nature of reality and justify their authenticity or irregularity. No more can anyone deceive us as to what is

72

real. Yet, it rests upon ourselves to do the work and make the effort. No other can establish an acquaintance with the nature of the incorporeal imminence but ourselves because it requires that the human, essential identity assert itself within the human constitution in order that phenomena may be directly encountered and definitively identified. We must engage circumstances immediately from the perspective of the human, essential identity in order to know them for what they actually are.

Immediately experiencing our own individuality through direct cognition, and consequently, recognizing the incorporeal nature of our existence, we determine that we are comparable in essence to the identity of all other people. Yet, we are also individually unique. The distinction between ourselves and others lies with our own intrinsic singularity of existence.

Upon death, the body disintegrates but human existence continues incorporeally. There is no interruption. The human, intrinsic identity exists in a condition of unique distinction. It is the immutable human, essential existence that recognizes the similarly incorporeal distinctions that intrinsically identify phenomena.

6. QUALITATIVE EXISTENTIAL EXPRESSION

The apprehension of the essential identity of a phenomenon reveals that intrinsic distinction exists intangibly and beyond the capacity of empirical justification. The constitutional inherency that intrinsically identifies a thing cannot be definitively demonstrated as existent merely through abstract deduction but it is recognized through immediate engagement. This is because the intrinsic distinction of a phenomenon is not revealed through the physical appearance but discovered as its essential significance.

The physical properties of something are readily assessed by our conventional cognition and evaluated through reason. They are thought to represent the entirety of an object, but they only reveal a superficial perspective of it and not its intrinsic existence.

Experientially, the essential identity of a phenomenon is discovered as the qualitative significance of its existence. It is recognized through direct cognition that the essential existence of a person or of an object is of greater moment than the material appearance or the physical properties. The appearance of something or someone varies while the essential identity remains consistent.

It is from this perspective that the significant existence of organic forms is discovered not through peripheral examination, but through the manner whereby the creature expresses its existence and consequently identifies itself.

Clearly this position is at odds with the conventional approach. But it may be reasonably conceded that the appearance of another human being underlies a more significant identity. The body that changes over the course of time and events, scarcely represents the person who we have grown to recognize for their intrinsic existence and who we have come to regard. The superficial appearance misrepresents the individual. If this premise is further extended to encompass all phenomena alive and inanimate, it becomes clear that the appearance is a guise of an essential distinction that is recognized as authentic through the aegis of our own intrinsic nature.

It is pointless to commence an investigation of any nature from a position of prejudice. It merely results in the greater entrenchment, through determined polemic, of an already established perspective. Direct, experiential cognition avoids the bias of preconceptions altogether because it involves an immediate engagement with a phenomenon by the human quintessence. Prejudice always accompanies cerebral appraisal because rationalism is an indefinite practice of cognition. It is evaluative. Sentimental preference is similarly unreliable as it is an obviously fickle assessment founded upon preference. We avoid intermediary interpretations, preconceived positions and the tendency to return to already established evaluations of familiar circumstances, by the direct engagement through our authentic identity, with the phenomenon itself.

Materialistic, Western philosophy commences an evaluation of a situation from a determined and intractable approach founded upon the conviction that physical evidence alone comprises reality. This position is compounded through an extensive, abstract rationalism that interprets phenomena exclusively in material terms.

Perceptual prejudice abounds in many forms. It is direct cognition that is the rarity. Any pre-established position will be estranged from reality by virtue of its already, remotely structured condition. The intrinsic authenticity of something is only recognized through immediate experience and it is justified as authentic through the direct engagement of the human intrinsic identity with the phenomenon itself.

Intrinsic authenticity requires direct experience in order to be recognized because it is an immediate condition of existence that cannot be demonstrated as extant through rationalism. The condition of actuality is only qualified as existent through immediate engagement. Reality is either directly engaged or it remains an unknown condition. It is only experientially recognized and, consequently, it remains elusive to reason and abstract dialectic. Reality is the condition of existence wherein the authentic and essential identity of the human being resides. Consequently, immediate engagement reveals that which actually exists while rationalism calculates and deduces indirectly, striving to evaluate situations through a scrutiny of the physical properties and the contextual circumstances of a phenomenon. Reality is a condition of actuality discovered through immediate engagement and experientially qualified by the human, essential identity which exists immanently within it. The experientially recognized circumstance of the immediate existence of the human, essential identity becomes the standard or measure whereby an assertion may be authenticated as either real or fictitious.

Authenticity is a qualitative condition that, as a value, is entirely intangible. Actuality as a state cannot be assessed through abstract rationalism because reason functions logically and argues between the truth of an exposition and an erroneous postulate, through deduction. The reality of something is its qualitative condition of authenticity. Just as quantity and quality are incommensurate values, similarly, reality is a condition or status that cannot be calculated and argued. Alike to all other intangible conditions that qualify phenomena, reality must be experienced in order to be recognized.

There is an assumption of having attained definitive knowledge when the exclusively material appearances of an organism are sufficiently scrutinized and when their physical activities are recognized and isolated. The creature is evaluated upon its appearance and analyzed for its mechanical, electrical and chemical activity in the attempt to determine what its essential existence. But naming myriad isolated parts, functions and the constitution of tissue merely offers detailed information concerning an object's physical appearance. It cannot reveal the significance that distinguishes one creature from another because identity is intrinsically established and does not exist peripherally.

The distinction between two creatures does not reside conclusively with the appearance. The essential identity of a creature exists in the manner whereby the commonalities of animal or plant construction are qualitatively expressed. The quality of the expression of a creature is intrinsic and, as such, it is only recognized through immediate, experiential cognition. While differences remain physically evident, the intrinsic, qualitative identity is essential and recognized as the authentic distinction between creatures.

Direct engagement is a qualitatively juxtaposed practice to abstract rationalism. A phenomenon is known originally through our human, essential identity and discovered for what it is through an immediacy of experience. The object is not merely physically evaluated but encountered instantly and distinguished by its quality of distinction, which is its authentic identity.

All flora is recognized as such, through the commonalities of appearance that they share. It is the qualitative manner whereby these similarities are particularly represented that reveals the essential distinction between two plants. The essential difference is not exclusive to the appearance, but it is a qualitative distinction. The same applies to animals. They are distinguished by the qualitative manner of their expression which is revealed to the observer through immediate engagement in much the same way as a master artist discovers and represents the essential of a subject.

Materialism resists this position because it is imagined that direct cognition is less objective than material scrutiny. But the exclusive preoccupation with the appearances of things fails to reveal their intrinsic condition and the essential nature of their existence. They can never be essentially identified through an exclusive consideration of their superficial and transient semblances.

The manner whereby the intrinsic identity of a phenomenon, the value of a philosophical stance towards life or a belief system may be evaluated for its authenticity, resides with immediate experience. This is because immediacy involves essential experience and not merely superficial evaluation. A preferred perspective of evaluation, whether it champions materialism or a religious position, may be argued convincingly and endlessly in support or contradiction. Unless something is engaged through direct cognition by the human, essential identity, its intrinsic existence cannot be definitively determined.

Through mathematics the exclusively quantifiable properties of an object may be calculated and manipulated, but they fail to represent the entirety or the essential distinction of the object. Intangible values, qualities and intrinsic natures are completely neglected because they cannot be numerically represented with any reasonable justice. The object is reduced to an abstract framework solely represented by the measurable characteristics of its physical appearance.

Similarly, chemical interactions are represented less by the manner whereby one essential, qualitative identity engages another but by abstract values. However, the occurrence of a chemical reaction between the qualitative distinctions of chemicals is correctly recognized when they are immediately identified for their intrinsic natures.

The occurrence of electrical phenomena in organisms similarly indicates the essential workings but is vastly remote from a recognition of their inherent identity. The intrinsic significance of physically apparent phenomena resides with their essential, qualitative distinction and not within the physical appearance.

The condition of reality is experientially known through an immediate encounter and consists of extant, qualitative distinctions that are the authentic identities beyond physical appraisal. In the condition of reality, phenomena possess inherent identity that qualitatively identifies them. Direct engagement does not involve the intellect nor appraisal by the human, feeling nature. The authentic human identity, that remains when dialectical and sentimental evaluation is suspended, experiences a phenomenon immediately. The human, essential singularity is our own intrinsic identity and the necessary foundation of the immediate engagement, and consequent experience, of the significant distinction between phenomena.

Whenever we come across a perspective that is unfamiliar and unconventional, we endeavor to define, categorize and finally dispense with it, imagining that we have it tidily compartmentalized if it somehow resembles and corresponds with our established convictions. We consider ourselves informed and dismiss further exploration as unnecessary. Once the novel approach is classified in an orderly fashion we feel more secure because now we can evaluate it abstractly against our previously established views. It is very difficult for us to explore something originally without reference to formerly accepted certainties. The confidence whereby we evaluate something is constituted upon earlier formulation. However, we have the inherent capacity as human beings to know things directly and uniquely without reliance upon accumulated concepts. The human, essential identity engages phenomena in the immediate manner of experiential cognition. This allows us to approach the irregular as if it were unknown and in terms of its singularity. The authentic identity of the human being explores phenomena as they are, elementally, untrammeled by comparison with prior assessments. The authentic identity of an object is determined through an immediate encounter. Through the direct, cognitive approach, it is known for its essential significance. Thus, we avoid prejudice. The phenomenon is instead recognized for its unique qualitative identity and the distinction of its intrinsic nature.

The direct approach towards existence yields intelligence of a different caliber to the conventional, materialistic perspective. Theoretical constructs, that have arisen through an exclusive accentuation of physical appearances and properties, do not assist in definitive identification because reason and postulation offer only an oblique approach, incommensurate with the discovery of the essential condition of a phenomenon. In order to definitively determine, if something exists it must be immediately experienced. The essential condition of phenomenal existence is discovered only through experience because is a state of existence or unreality. While rationalism evaluates information concerning physical functions, it cannot explicitly substantiate the existence or absence of existence because it is an indirect function.

The conventional, theoretical approach towards existence, while empirically established, yet relies exclusively upon materially justified data. An alternative conviction that requires belief, is equally indefensible because its legitimacy is unverifiable and must be accepted on trust. Theoretical positions, whether conventional or alternative that rely upon the consensus of a scholarly elite, remain credible only through our confidence in the reliability of the source and the persuasiveness of the reasoning.

The immediate approach is significant because it is without prejudice or preferential conviction. The crucial distinction between immediate cognition and all other approaches rests upon who it is who apprehends the phenomena. The essential identity and not the apparent significance of the human being, exists in an elemental or original condition. Consequently, it engages the similarly essential condition of everything that it encounters.

The apparent identity of the human being is corporeal and epitomized as the brain. The brain functions intellectually but the condition of reality is indiscoverable through calculation. Essential, human existence, however, is incorporeal and engages phenomena in the condition of their intrinsic existence.

Abstract rationalism fabricates plausible solutions to problems based upon materially founded information. The popular theory of evolution is a case in point. It remains a theory because as a construct, it can never be demonstrated as authentic. It is the highest endeavor of reason but it is not definitive intelligence. The popular concept of an evolutionary complex of life-forms arising from a primitive progenitor is recognized as an abstract fallacy when phenomena are instead explored through direct cognition. This is because we examine the occurrence of the living organism immediately and originally, without attempting to rationalize it. We wish to discover what it is and not merely how it works. Consequently, we do not confuse function with identity. Through intrinsic identification we find no necessity to establish a theoretical construct to explain the appearance of organisms nor do we attribute purpose to their particular, physical traits. The physical traits of creatures are not necessarily purposeful. The horn of a rhino or the antlers of a moose are not devices or implements but extensions of the demeanor and consequent form expression of the particular creature. Recognizing their intrinsic identities, we discover that the distinctions between creatures conform to the qualitative manner of their physical expression. The creature is identified less through its appearance and more significantly by the manner of its essential expression.

The identification of a creature for its qualitative significance through immediate experience, reveals the evolutionary theory as it currently stands, as untenable because it fails to recognize what it is that essentially differentiates one organism from another. It is the qualitatively distinct expression that determines identity and consequent appearance. The appearance of a creature is a cumulative consequence of the changing quality of its nature, over time.

Even through conventional rationalism, capricious evolution from simplicity to complexity is an extraordinary overreach of credibility. Sophistication does not develop from simplicity, crude organization or from capricious, physical forces. A living form of greater significance does not have a rudimentary genesis. Even abstractly considered, the progenitor must embody in principle, the entire range of the diversity of the descendants. Primordially, the progenitor is recognized as an archetypal, conceptual arrangement according to which, every expression must remain consistent in principle, in order to function. Organisms vary in the qualitative manner of their expression but remain essentially consistent to their conceptual origins. The manner whereby an organism is expressed, changes through response to ecological divergence which, consequently influences the appearance of the creature. Thus, the term evolution is recognized to be a misnomer in the manner in which it is ordinarily understood.

7. QUALITATIVE DIFFERENTIATION

The antecedent of the contemporary creature is neither simple nor primitive. It is a conceptualization consisting of a complexity of interrelationships establish towards the achievement of a particular end. The archetype is the ideal working-epitome upon which all organic expressions are established and according to which they must always stay consistent in order to remain viable. An archetype consists of a compound of complex intricacy whereby an animated, functioning structure is achieved through the continual metamorphic reapplication of living substance. It is the ideal blueprint or systemic paradigm according to which living organisms are intrinsically established.

A creature possesses a conceptual ideal and a particular intonation according to cumulative qualitative divergences of emphasis. The universal, conceptual ideal is qualitatively expressed. Two creatures differ essentially according to their cumulative nature which is, subsequently revealed through the appearance.

The consistencies and commonalities between two plants identify them as flora. We recognize all plants immediately because they possess a familiar and archetypal organization which determines them as plants. However, the distinction between two plants is qualitative in that one flower, leaf or seed differs from that of another plant by virtue of the character of its expression.

87

The qualitative disposition that distinguishes one plant from another exists consistently throughout every detail and iota of the plant and identifies it. The Archetype remains consistent while the nature of the plant varies.

The distinction between the animal and the human being lies in the manner whereby a shared animalian archetype is expressed. The archetype remains consistent, alike to that peculiar to the plant kingdom. Again the animal is qualitatively differentiated according to a cumulative demeanor or stance towards the ecological conditions in which it finds itself. However, the human form approximates the original archetype with very little variation even though the human experiences a wide variety of temperamental combinations and variations. The human form continues to resemble the archetype and is only very superficially divergent in appearance.

Archetypes are complex and intricate conceptions that are realized as organic life under the different vivifying qualities inherent to the Agencies of water, air, sunlight and warmth. The archetype is expressed physically through the organization of biomaterial substance. Biomaterial substance is living tissue without particularity or characteristic identity. It is vivified by the influence of the four Agencies. The archetype is recognized throughout the progressive, metamorphic cycle of appearances and functions, as the procedural entirety. Organic life diversifies and occupies ecosystems through an adaption of demeanor. Creatures become alike to their ecological contexts.

The archetypes may exist essentially without being physically realized, but they must remain simultaneously united with biomaterial and the Agencies or organic life ceases to exist. If the influence of even one the Agencies was entirely withheld from an organic life the archetype would become moot and biomaterial would be undefined. If the archetype itself were withdrawn organic life would become an application without conceptual organization. Biomaterial would consequently be rendered structureless and aimless. Therefore, it is recognized that the archetype, biomaterial and the Agencies must have existed together in tandem, from the foundation of organic life upon Earth.

The seed of a tree such as the easily identified acorn or walnut remains characteristically entirely oak or walnut-like. Seeds are the epitome of the tree in seed form but instead of expressing the mature tree expansively, it is revealed in an entirely concentrated manner. The shell has, in some variations, a leaf-like texture, while in others it resembles bark, that instead of being linearly or radially expressed is now intensified in the round. Even the surface of the acorn cupule often shows a distinctly rounded, bark-like texture out of which the seed is produced as a concentration of the entirety.

The seed is an alternative expression of the entire, tree identity that, as the acorn, is represented differently in form but remains essentially and qualitatively consistent. The oak does not produce the acorn as an aspect of itself. The intrinsic, characteristic nature of the oak is revealed, through metamorphic reappearance according to the archetypal dictate, as a particular seed. The seed is the reappearance of the identical, tree nature, transformed metamorphically according to the demands of the life cycle. This occurs in compliance with the archetypal tree concept and is distinguished according to the distinct nature whereby the individual tree is interpreted. Thus, we once again catch a glimpse of the working of the archetype and glean something of its genius.

The archetype, as the ideal, primordial progenitor, develops variations in the quality whereby it is expressed but its descendants do not develop or evolve greater complexity. They merely vary according to the manner of their characteristic demeanor and temperament. The plasticity of form appearance that we recognize is the consequence of cumulative changes in qualitative demeanor. Forms vary through a dynamic of historical metamorphosis from the undefined expression of the archetype into the specific and specialized appearance. Organisms remain the same in principle, true to the archetype, but they possess a plasticity in the tenor of their essential quality of expression. The characteristic expression adjusts according to responses to ecological challenges. Their particularistic nature alters and, subsequently, their appearance adjusts accordingly.

While alterations in essential identity have a cumulative influence upon appearances, contemporary adjustments only influence the existing arrangement of the archetypal expression. Creatures do not regress to an earlier form but reform the extant, physical arrangement, according to changes in their demeanor. Form alters at the expense of the existing, physical condition. Prior forms are steadily relinquished. There is no reversal to an earlier entirety of appearance because the contemporary form no longer retains the ancestral formulation. This is because a certain propensity of demeanor becomes emphasized in form expression according to the nature of the creature's extant condition. The reconstituted appearance embodies the accentuation as if it were original because the entirety, and not just an isolated attribute, is reworked. Further adjustment effects only the present condition and not the state of the ancestral expression because the original establishment no longer exists. Only the contemporary condition is subject to adjustment because nothing new is introduced through reconstitution. The extant condition is restructured according to a twist or reversal in temperament but originality only exists in terms of the manner of recombination.

In other words, the undistinguished, ancestral appearance is influenced by a change in the propensity and demeanor of the creature. That adjustment of qualitative identity is a temperamental response to ecological challenge. Countless generations later a creature may respond to ecological challenge in exactly the same manner as its forbears did ancestrally. But now the change in the propensity and demeanor alters the extant form as it presently exists within the confines of accumulated and particular parameters of distinction. Again, this is because the entirety of a form, in its present condition, is reworked. Change does not occur merely in the isolated detail. Changes in the qualitative, essential identity that distinguishes a creature occur, not merely in the limb or the head but the entirety itself is always refashioned according to a different, temperamentally induced emphasis. The equilibrium of the form is reestablished according to the criteria of the archetype but with a revised quality of expression. Every organic expression always embodies the entirety of the archetype while the temperament of creatures and their appearances correspond with one another qualitatively. With every change in demeanor, the reworked entirety becomes the new foundation of subsequent alteration.

Vegetation alters directly through the influence of a compound and variable ecology. Plant life becomes alike to the qualitative condition of its ecological context and adjusts cumulatively, in its entirety, without regression to a former condition. While the working conception of the plant always remains archetypal, buffeted and challenged by myriad historical, ecological demands, the manner in which the archetype is represented is compounded, adjustment upon adjustment. But equilibrium is always reestablished with every generation. A plant always essentially remains a plant. This is because the archetype is a conceptual complexity that must exist in its entirety in order that the organism remains tenable. A single aspect cannot change in isolation, or the entirety becomes unworkable.

Forms develop with increasingly distinct, qualitative characteristics that are reflected in their appearances. Flora is progressively restricted and frequently suited only to a particular, ecological context. The options of further significant change narrow cumulatively because earlier formations no longer exist and the existing structure becomes the basis of any re-emphasis. Trees and plants alter qualitatively after the nature of the ecological context. They become unavoidably restricted to optimal ecological conditions that are specific to the cumulative diversity of their modifications. They inevitably became increasingly inflexible in nature and form because each qualitative alteration is established upon the immediately prior condition.

A jungle vine, prolific, climbing, broad of leaf, in forest shade and damp, in nature alike to the jungle itself, is severely challenged when its optimum ecology alters to sun-bleached aridity. In the unlikely event that it does not perish entirely, it becomes the same vine but now reduced in leaf and succulence. The jungle vine has taken on the nature of the new conditions.

A particular qualitative nature, established alike to the character of an ecological context, is challenged through ecological variance. The possibility of physical reinterpretation is narrowed increasingly because only an already established condition is reworked. Qualitative adjustment, that primordially would have been enormously significant, can now only influence appearances very slightly. Consequently, the occurrence of a severe ecological challenge today would, in most cases, result in certain extinction.

In animals, any alteration of the qualitative interpretation of the archetype occurs through adjustments in disposition because they are feeling sentient. The demeanor responds to the circumstances of ecology that challenge or mollify it. This dynamic occurs constantly, and the demeanor is continually influenced and cumulatively altered in response to challenge. Altered circumstances require the creature to adapt behaviorally and temperamentally. A behavioral adaption that changes the character of the creature provokes a form variation because form and nature are in a corresponding relationship. Conversely, the demeanor of a creature is also reciprocally influenced by its inherited condition. Thus, the range within which a form may alter according to an adjustment in demeanor is limited within the confines of the cumulatively, inherited restrictions born of variations in temperamental emphasis.

Vegetation is distinguished according to the characteristic manner whereby it expresses the archetypal plant through the direct impact of the ecology. The character of a plant is directly crafted by the quality of the ecology and plant and context tend to become alike in nature.

But animals are differentiated in appearance indirectly, according to the sentient nature of their response to influence. In our time, animals no longer possess the option to dramatically rebuild because an alteration in demeanor only influences the established condition. Physical change now occurs within the constituted definition even though the demeanor of a creature may alter considerably. Thus, the domestication of the progenitor of the present-day gray wolf was a severe ecological modification. Dogs vary enormously in appearance because of temperamental diversity compounded through cumulative, selective breeding based upon both disposition and physical attributes. While enormous superficial variation is evident, essentially all breeds remain dogs. There is no possibility for them to become different species because of the extreme narrowness of definition produced through form specificity. They no longer have a general, undifferentiated potential but alter only within the narrow parameters of the current form. The current form is the new original. They can change qualitatively within their current specification but their primordial, general form has been superseded by the very specific. The former indefiniteness no longer exists.

The temperament of a creature is variable. It changes in response to ecological influence. Upon reproduction, an altered disposition influences the form emphasis. While demeanor continues to fluctuate depending upon ecological circumstances, the manner of its influence is confined within the terms of the existing form condition. Changes in temperament may be dramatic, as in the case of domestication, but the scope of form change is narrowed through accumulated distinction.

An animal's distinction is the cumulative manner whereby the ideal conception or archetype is qualitatively expressed. When variations arise, they are not capricious and unpredictable but the consequences of an alteration in the nature of a creature in response to ecological modification. They are not erratic mutations. Darwin failed to recognize the reciprocal relationship between temperament and form and overlooked the dynamic whereby an alteration in demeanor provokes a different form emphasis. The observations that he made concerning animal husbandry and the crossing of different breeds for their advantageous traits, obscured the fact that variations had arisen in the first place, because of the changes in ecology that domestication implied. Where domestic animals were selected and bred for appearance, they were also, unbeknownst, selected for temperament even if this was not the primary intention.

Lifeforms possess a plasticity of demeanor and consequent appearance. The response to ecological circumstances provokes an alteration in the disposition of the animal. Disposition precedes appearance, and the form peculiarity of the animal is redirected through a different emphasis of character and demeanor towards an alternative physical gesture of form. Variations do not occur in isolation but the impulse towards a different temperament, appearing as a potential physical change, causes the entire form composition of the creature to be reworked according to a particular qualitative emphasis. Accordingly, the creature's appearance adjusts in concession to a different propensity of nature and demeanor that alters the characteristic manner whereby form is composed. The qualitative gesture of the creature towards life is a significance that applies to its form entirety. Thus, an emphasis that blatantly exaggerates one aspect of the creature over another will correspondingly alters every other detail and aspect. The whole creature will be true in gesture to the newly established demeanor that is introduced into its heredity through reproduction.

It is well known that form variations begin to arise upon the isolation of a portion of an animal population. The ecological dynamic is particularly altered with respect to numerical intensity, and its consequences must influence demeanor and, inevitably, also the physical appearance of the creatures. The isolated group becomes an alternative population in the making, existing under an altered dynamic of influences.

In terms of the mineral kingdom, the distinction between elements is also qualitatively significant. But their intrinsic identities do not change unless they react with one another and become, through combination, not an aggregate but an entirely new entity of a different quality and nature altogether. The new identity, for example, might be explosive, poisonous or in some other fashion qualitatively distinct from the original elements or compounds.

The human being embodies much of the animal condition with the inclusion of an intrinsic, individual distinction. The human composition is enhanced and elevated by the addition of the eternal, incorporeal, essential identity which is our authentic significance and the authority of our human constitution.

The authentic condition of things becomes directly known when the human, essential identity encounters phenomena immediately. The legitimate status of things is recognized through direct experience. Knowledge of a considerably greater dimension is achieved than could ever be attained through conventional abstract evaluation.

8. PURPOSEFUL ORGANIC INGENUITY

Conventionally, materialistic, Western philosophy approaches life through the preoccupation and scrutiny of the material circumstances and intricacies of phenomena. It is imagined that if we consolidate our conclusions we will arrive at a judicious understanding of our human selves and the world, discovering an acceptable rationale of the elaborate perplexities of existence.

The popular idea is that the world and all it contains consists of diminutive, anonymous building blocks of matter that somehow amalgamate and congeal in orderly arrangements under the impetus of uncreative forces. However, experiential, direct cognition reveals that existence is composed only of entireties. Furthermore, we find that the characteristic nature of the whole is distinctly different from the identity of the minutia. The subsequent, philosophical disparity arises from the differing points of view of alternative disciplines. The former is conceptual while the direct approach is empirical. Consequently, a material analysis will inevitably fail to reveal the significance of entireties because it isolates physical components but neglects the imperative of formative incentive.

Similarly, the essential identity of a phenomenon is qualitative and intrinsic and does not reside in the physical properties themselves, but it is implied substantively by the particular nature of the appearance.

The abstract, materialistic approach towards understanding existence, has become doctrinally established as the predominant methodology because it seems unproblematic. However, scientific discipline is inevitably exclusive because it fails when applied to incommensurate, incorporeal circumstances that exist elusively, except through implication. Unfortunately, a selective mind that only considers the obvious as authentic, does not readily pursue inferences particularly if they indicate physically intangible volition. Therefore, the entrenched, materialistic perspective is effortlessly maintained because it is interminable and self-sustaining, while the suggestion that there may exist an integral wisdom beyond obsessive materialism, is an easily forestalled dissent.

Notwithstanding, if we proceed with courage and explore the world and the condition of our existence through the approach of original cognition, we quickly discover that, contrary to conventional opinion, existence is not entirely physical. The elementary building block theory does not contain within it an explanation of the conceptual impetus of living organization. Neither do the capricious influences of physical forces upon inanimate material possess the capacity to establish progressive consolidation. In other words, the difference between disorder and arrangement rests upon the manner of the configuration that causes things to work. Therefore, we must realistically search for the incentive for physical aggregation and not pretend that creation could have occurred by happenstance over millennia of chaotic disorder.

The conviction that significance is revealed through exhaustive reduction of the detail may be distantly attributed to the writings of René Descartes (1596 – 1650). But analysis is indicative of a determined materialistic preoccupation that ensures that the Cartesian perspective remains entrenched. Research into the subtleties and minutiae that comprise the phenomenal instant continues unabated in the conviction that everything concerning life and the universe will be satisfactorily understood to the degree that the mechanical, chemical and electrical properties of any sample of matter are isolated and identified.

However, the abstract belief that the totality of a phenomenon resides within the material particulars is unfounded in reality. Obviously, the properties of fundamental building blocks may be reactive but they are not endowed with constructive organization. Furthermore, the greater the material reduction, the more estranged from the entirety the components become. That is to say, dissociated building blocks lose the significance that they possessed as a configuration.

Similarly, the behavior of inorganic substances is inflexibly predictable according to the characteristic nature of the mineral concerned. Thereby, physical and electro-magnetic forces operate as expected within the parameters of specific circumstances. But while the properties of matter and physical forces substantially comprise phenomena, they remain intrinsically without ingenuity and without the capacity of conceptualization. They are essentially involuntary and incapable of intentional organization. That is to say, they will always operate according to character.

Correspondingly, working, organic organization cannot be adequately explained in mechanical terms from the properties of either an organ of a creature or from the genetic chronicle. When we observe complex systems, whereby, organisms entirely transform in order to achieve a specific end, energy is undoubtedly in evidence, but it is concerted and by no means random. Furthermore, creatures exist that arrange and conduct complex form metamorphosis whereby an unprecedented, living condition is established from a previous, entirely opposite arrangement. In other words, when the organizational motive is imperceptible from a scrutiny of the physical substances and forces, the required creative mind must exist elusively.

Original observation without pre-conceptional bias reveals that the intrinsic significance of a living and functioning creature lies both in the foundational concept that anticipates it, and the manner whereby it is particularly represented. While unrecognizable, as such, from a scrutiny of the minutiae of the parts, nevertheless,

102

the organic concept exists as an ingenious formulation, while the sophisticated organization of an organism ensures practical viability. Furthermore, we subsequently recognize the industry of genius through the aptitude with which the same intrinsic functions and procedures work towards a very specific end.

Inevitably, we must conclude that extremely sophisticated, living structures do not occur spontaneously even upon a timescale of infinity. Therefore, if for a moment, we would restrain abstract speculation and engage circumstances originally without farfetched presumption, we would discern these things straightforwardly for ourselves.

Without doubt, the abstract consideration and evaluation of the exclusively material conditions of existence advance a narrow perspective. Further, if an aspect of a situation is isolated and contemplated in an attempt to discover its secrets, and the findings philosophically extrapolated to encompass the entirety, our understanding of life will be nonsensical. Indeed, the approach to understanding is backwards if, in our research, we compromise the integrity of the prevailing circumstances. Conversely, if through original, impartial engagement, we directly contemplate the undiminished conditions of a phenomenon, inevitably the intrinsic expression itself becomes evident.

Further, understanding is frequently, unavoidably prejudiced through the perspective of specialized scholarship. Accordingly, life is explored upon the basis of the mechanics, mathematics or the chemistry of things, the results will be correspondingly characteristic. Meanwhile, the particular nature of the expression of a phenomenon remains unknown because that distinction is only grasped when the entirety is directly engaged.

Unless a thing is considered in its entirety the intrinsic significance remains essentially unrecognized. In order to grasp what something is it must be engaged in the condition of its completeness. Similarly, in order to understand organic life an aggregate of separate parts will not do because through analysis, all the parts will have been allotted separate significance and the identity of the whole phenomenon overlooked. Needless to say, it is impossible to reassemble all the separate iotas of information regarding a phenomenon because only the seemingly pertinent will be selected. The resulting understanding will be distorted through preference and priority, and as stated previously, every phenomenal aspect will be examined according to different specialties of learning.

Reductionism as an approach towards understanding a whole phenomena is inevitably an unproductive practice because it involves the examination of particular details one at a time. The scrutiny of an assortment of separate aspects and properties of a phenomenon will inevitably mislead the researcher into imagining that the identity of the entirety is understood through the significance of separate details.

René Descartes advocated the reductionist methodology towards understanding because he thought that circumstances might be better understood piecemeal that as an insurmountable problem. However, the preferred approach should depend upon the objective. If we wish to know how a thing works gradual analysis will reveal the laws of physics whereby it operates. But if we desire to know what something is we need to discern the intrinsic significance and characteristic nature that describes it.

In other words, engineering and mathematics deal exclusively with attributes that can be understood in those particular terms and can be further reduced through quantification, and if desired, represented according to the numerical value distilled from their material conditions. This has nothing to do with intrinsic identity but merely corresponds with the physical, chemical or electrical aspects. That is to say, the intrinsic identifier is qualitatively explicit but epitomized through the expression of the entirety, and consequently, it is essentially irreducible.

In order to identify what a phenomenon intrinsically is, in its own right, the particularity cannot be established abstractly or upon the strength of the obvious, physical properties, but it must be discerned through immediate cognition. In much the same way, we do another human being an injustice if we confuse the biological vehicle with the host.

Obviously, the physical is real, but in terms of essential conditions the body is a superficial representation, and not the innate person. If we engage other people depending solely upon their appearance our correspondence will be correspondingly shallow. Nevertheless, the physical serves as focus of our attention whereby, through immediate cognition, we can discover the intrinsic singularity.

In everyday life, both human rationale and affective evaluation, is unbeknownst often involuntarily coupled with direct cognition whereby a fuller picture of the object of our attention is achieved. But in order to recognize and understand the greater significance of phenomena we can identify the essential importance purposefully through straightforward cognition.

Unfortunately, a cursory understanding of existence is the habitual approach and materialism has established a monopoly, so that a purely physical world-view has encroached upon, and distorted, our notion of reality, reducing all things to the extent of their obvious appearances. Consequently, the human being is similarly imagined to exist merely in physical terms.

Predictably, an exclusively materialistic mindset is a dead-end in terms of further human evolution because we require the perspective of the human, intrinsic singularity in order that phenomena may be intrinsically identified. Furthermore, if human beings continue to consider themselves corporeally circumscribed the incentive to strive towards a meaningful, principled ethos remains uncertain.

Nevertheless, whether we recognize it or not, there exists an essential, qualitative magnitude that underlies the mere appearance of things and gives meaning to the empty carapace. Consequently, the challenge of our time is to discover a realistic approach whereby each individual may discover the intrinsic nature of things for themselves.

We discover the human, essential ipseity through direct, experiential cognition. Thereupon, with the conventional, evaluative faculties conditionally restrained the individual can ascertain the substantive significance of all things. When the conventional approach to understanding is restrained, naturally, the essential identity of the human being assumes the seat of cognitive authority.

The error of evaluating existence exclusively upon the basis of the physical conditions is superseded through straightforward engagement. Thereby, qualitative distinction, essential individuality and intrinsic natures are recognized as the substantive foundation of the obvious appearance.

Upon this foundation, an appreciation for intrinsic significances is established and further accumulated through an adjustment of perspective from the superficial view to that of the human, essential distinction.

In other words, the human ipseity, experientially

aware of its own uniqueness, directly explores the circumstances in which it finds itself. It recognizes that the former, exclusively material perspective was construed and it now discerns the essential significance of things. Consequently, immediately engaging phenomena from the profound perspective of the individual, intrinsic selfhood, it recognizes them for their significance and qualitative dimensionality.

For example, we find that the immaculate manner whereby organic organization is devised is vastly purposeful and not simply coincidental as materialistic, Western philosophy would have us believe. In reality, even obvious biological intricacies such as the metamorphic reinterpretation of organic form are established towards a particular end. Indeed, we would have to deny our own observation to the contrary if we were to accept the concept of capricious origination and spontaneous upward progression as the authentic, operating modality of existence.

Direct, cognitive engagement through the human essence with an organic phenomenon, reveals the activities of conceptualization, volition and realization. Metamorphosis does not arise haphazardly out of physical circumstances and, organization is not produced through oblivious caprice. Ecological circumstances are influential to appearances, but they are not creative in themselves. They cannot produce organic systems because they do not possess volition nor intention. Their influences are random. Living organization of every nature is always purposeful in that it immaculately and repeatedly achieves a specific objective.

The objective of a living organization is revealed through its activity of growth. It moves metamorphically, through events and appearances towards a specific result. It grows through sequential expressions that metamorphose from one arrangement into another in order to establish a very specific and functioning system. Order and organization cannot arise from the inconstancy of physical forces because mechanical influence incorporates no such ingenuity. The resourcefulness of archetypal conceptualization, according to which an organic arrangement is established, is recognized when one engages a situation directly and refrains from abstract analysis and conjecture.

It is typical of the indirect approach that we avoid a first-hand encounter with a situation in order to determine what it is of itself and, instead, indulge our own interpretation of what a phenomenon must be. We imagine that what we think about something is more meaningful that what it, in fact, is. We do this because we are ignorant of the significance of the direct encounter. It is thought that the human explanation of something, carefully reasoned and systematically argued is an authority that supersedes in significance, the intrinsicality of the phenomenon itself.This is because we imagine that our intellectual approach is the highest manner of cognition.

Unfortunately, the intellect is constitutionally incapable of recognizing the human, essential singularity because our intrinsic identity is incorporeal. Intrinsic existence has no physical presence and consequently, reason finds nothing to engage except perhaps indirectly, by implication. But self-recognition of the human, essential identity is necessary in order that phenomena may be experienced for their intrinsic significance. Fortunately, while abstract rationalism cannot recognize incorporeal relevance, direct experience can experience it uniquely. The human, essential singularity can immediately know of its own authenticity and this throws open wide the door to a similarly direct cognition of all phenomena.

9. ATTRIBUTION

Without direct engagement from the perspective of our singular existence we rely merely upon oblique, cerebral evaluation. Consequently, we fail to attribute the organization of sophisticated, organic systems to genius because conventional cognition does not involve the immediate engagement of the intrinsic existence of phenomena, wherein genius is apparent. We imagine that organized and immaculate living systems with specific, purposeful consequences, capriciously arose. We think they developed and organized spontaneously because we cannot discern the presence of incorporeal significances through abstract rationalism and we imagine that they are merely, implied or invented. Yet, the contrary hypothesis of impulsive, self-organization beggars belief until the conjectural contradiction of immaculate, though arbitrary arrangement, is qualified by the introduction of a new value: infinite time. Content with this structure we rest secure and imagine that we know something.

Abstraction can never definitively achieve authentic knowledge of phenomenal reality because it remains indirect however resourcefully the intellect may rearrange and calculate information. Further, the manner whereby a situation is evaluated remotely from the immediate experience cannot escape prejudice. It is a shallow and distinctly biased position that contends that organic organization is the consequence of lifeless influences. It is ridiculed when the situation is directly and immanently engaged. Frequently, these unreasonable positions are fueled by an anxiety against the introduction of unsubstantiated belief or faith in something whose existence is rationally unjustifiable from a consideration of solely, material evidence. It is imagined that the materialistic approach is the opposite of belief and faith while in fact they resemble each other remarkably closely.

The materialistic systems conceived by theorists are profoundly at odds with what is known through direct cognition. The distinction between abstract conceptualization and knowledge achieved through the engagement of the human essence with a phenomenon, by immediate experience, is qualitative. They are incommensurable activities. The intellect is of a specific and very singular nature in that it abstractly calculates. The human essence engages the phenomenon directly and experiences it for what it is. Henri-Louis Bergson (1859 – 1941) applied his formidable intellect towards deciphering the riddle of human existence and comprehending the world. Although he discussed the cognitive practice of immediate experience and intuition, it would appear from his writings that his conclusions were arrived at intellectually. Bergson's approach was academic not experiential. He neglected to differentiate between abstract reasoning, and intelligence discovered through the direct engagement of the human essence.

Yet, he wrote of it as if he did. In order to address all the aspects of existence under one system, he found the need to identify life itself, but it remained only an abstract concept because he failed to discern its physical presence. He reasoned that by implication there must exist a life-endowing agency but he was unable to determine it. Consequently, he felt compelled to invent what he imagined should exist and he named that which vivifies matter Élan vital.

This contrived conjecture is entirely typical of the manner whereby the intellect functions. It endeavors to establish a universal structure that explains everything. When that system fails to embrace all the facts then another value is introduced that addresses the insufficiency and the formulation is once again, viably established. The abstract approach always follows a similar routine regardless of the subject under consideration.

Unfortunately, an abstract fabrication, however masterfully it may be conceived, is not qualitatively compatible with directly experienced actuality. It will always remain contrived because of the indirect manner of its establishment. When the world is immediately engaged by the human essence the authentic disposition of things become directly known. They do not have to be interpreted nor abstractly reasoned. An artificial structure is not required in order to explain a phenomenon that is directly apprehended, because it is recognized in its

113

original and authentic condition through the immediacy of the engagement.

Had Bergson actually practiced what he called immediate experience and intuition he would have recognized that his entire conjectural approach was essentially abstract. Direct engagement through the aegis of the human, essential singularity enables us to experientially know the intrinsic identity of phenomena. Bergson would have found no necessity to fabricate the existence of Élan vital but would have discovered its authenticity as the essential, qualitative reality of the Agencies of life: air, sunlight, warmth and water. Thus, he took the concept immediate experience and intuition as his shibboleth but pursued his philosophical position intellectually.

Bergson ceded to the existence of the vitality of nature but he could not physically justify it. He reasoned its existence intellectually and further, named it, without actually localizing it. He realized the pertinence of vivification because without life organisms would remain inanimate. Yet, he did not know where or what it was. He merely recognized that it should be there, somewhere. He did not know what it was that vivified because it required immediate experience and intuition to know it. Similarly, he did not recognize the genius of organic organization except as another necessity of his abstract approach.

The discrepancy between intellectual conceptualization and immediately experienced reality is the result of the conflicting nature of two incommensurable, cognitive approaches. Incorporeal realities cannot be determined except by direct cognition because they lack physicality. Bergson reached as far as he possibly could abstractly in order to give credence to life, but he failed because knowledge concerning incorporeal significances is only achieved through direct, cognitive engagement.

The materialist attributes vitality and organization to physical influences, yet fails to explain what the actual forces are that produce life. It is imagined that life is a reaction to electricity, chemistry or physical influences. But it is generally and correctly conceded that air, water, warmth and sunlight sustain life but it is not known how they enliven. This is because the Agencies of life are recognized by the materialist, merely for the materially evident properties. They are unknown for their intangible, qualitative natures. But it is the intangible, qualitative distinctions and not solely the physical properties of air, water, warmth and sunlight, that are able to enliven. The incorporeal significances of the Agencies possess the capacity to enliven organic organization each according to its nature.

Thus, we recognize in nature, an over exposure to warmth and the effect of a dearth of water upon denizens of the desert. Similarly, when the air thins and warmth is insufficient with increased altitude, the flora of the mountainside appears stunted, woody and creeps close to the surface, tightly clinging to the earth. In deep caverns, where water is plentiful, but warmth, light and air are scarce, creatures become transparent and blind. The inequality of influence between the distinct, qualitative dispositions of the four Agencies is a significant, ecological consideration influencing organic expression.

Life is physically unrecognizable except through the presence or absence of the influence of the Agencies upon an organism. Intellectually, it is not known what life actually is, although it is erroneously suspected of establishing complex, organic organization. Thus, it is believed that if the ingredients of rudimentary protein are amalgamated, life will organize them into eventual complexity. But the enlivening qualities of air, water, warmth and sunlight do not themselves establish organization. They merely vivify. The Élan vital that Bergson theoretically identified resides as the essential identities of the Agencies of vivification. They are four qualitatively distinct and necessary elements. A complete deficiency of only one Agency and the organic form becomes unsustainable by the others, revealing both the collective significance of the Agencies and their unique, qualitative distinctions. The qualitatively distinct, vivifying influences of all four are required. Bergson failed to localize life because he was abstractly preoccupied. Immediate engagement alone, reveals the qualitative particularities and distinctions of the Agencies of life.

Similarly, the complexity of organic organization is

ingeniously and exclusively attributed to unsystematic, physical forces by materialistic, Western philosophy. Sophisticated and purposeful organic systems are not recognized as intentionally established but believed to have arisen miraculously through unrefined forces that, of themselves, possess no organization. Through such fiction materialism seeks to abstractly encompass all phenomenal organization.

Arising spontaneously from disorder organic organization, according to popular evolutionary theory, develops towards increasing complexity. Organic forms are supposed to produce chance variations unrelated to the ecological context of the creature. These are winnowed for suitability by capricious natural selection. Through spontaneous mutation organisms develop from simplicity to complexity. It is surmised that complex, organic intricacies arose from disorder by means of unpredictable, physical influences. Further, ecological caprice established the impetus towards complication including eventual intellectual development and self-consciousness.

The only rebuttal to a serious challenge against this unreasonable and contrived position is once more, the time value. It is supposed that absolutely anything may occur, including the impossible, if a sufficient span of time is allowed.

We cannot attribute organic organization to the Agencies that vivify and maintain animation and certainly not to lifeless physical influences that embody nothing of a comparable nature. The genius of organic organization is a vastly intricate and complex activity of metamorphosing re-expression towards a distinctly specific end. There is no qualitative relationship or similarity between unstructured, physical forces and multifaceted organization. Physical forces do not contain the capacity to establish sequentially developing arrangements. If the enlivening influence of the Agencies were to cease, the organism would simply collapse and disintegrate. The physical context would be of no constructive assistance at all. Similarly, if the organization were less than ideal it would fail to function then there would be nothing for the Agencies to animate. The Agencies and the viability of the organic organization must always exist in tandem. In terms of the living creature, the functioning arrangement and the four Agencies must be unfailingly, simultaneously apparent.

An organism is composed according to certain requirements. The archetype is a general, yet elaborate conception of considerable intricacy. It is the ideal basis according to which an organism must comply in order to be viable. It remains incorporeal, yet it is recognized through the manner of its specific application. The archetype exists, represented through countless variations of the same, elemental organization without being physically realized in its ideal condition. It is revealed solely through the diversity of its application.

Biomaterial is vivified and animated through the qualitative nature of the Agencies of air, water, sunlight and warmth. Without the agencies it dies and eventually becomes mineralized. Of itself, vivified biomaterial would have no order or structure. The archetype governs biomaterial purposefully requiring it to conform to the decrees of its very specific organization. Inherent to the archetypal dynamic is the capacity whereby decaying, unstructured biomaterial may be transformed through the agency of living biomaterial into the biochemical. Thus, we glimpse the extraordinary transformative capacity of biological organization.

The particular, characteristic manner whereby an organism, that would otherwise remain general and undifferentiated, is specifically realized, may be artistically described as its motif or the quality of its expression. It is the manner or nature whereby the ideal, archetypal construction is expressed, particularly. It is flexible by nature and its plasticity, evident through changing appearances, is both directly and circuitously influenced by ecology. Physical laws are complimented by localized influences that are qualitatively distinct. The compound ecology of the Earth determines the qualitative particularity and characteristic differentiation that distinguish one organism from another. The archetype is expressed as the essential plan and revealed through the metamorphic entirety of the organism. Without explicit expression or in the absence of a qualitative distinction, the archetype remains an unrealized, general conceptualization.

Lest this should seem a simplification, to the animal circumstance is added the feeling sentient nature which is the animal consciousness. Animal consciousness is not individual, but it exists as the collective identity of a population which, in turn, is of a quality consistently alike to the ideal, ecological context, to which the creature is bound as a qualitative extension. According to the condition of the animalian demeanor, the form appearance will adjust in character and gesture. Form variations arise as a consequence of the refashioned entirety, that adjusts according to the disposition and temperament of the creature. The creature will always incline qualitatively to its ecology.

Unlike the animal, the human being enjoys the potential of self-knowledge and upon this is established the possibility of singular autonomy.

When Bergson's immediate experience and intuition is practiced and not merely, formulaically presented as an intellectual construct, we engage phenomena directly without cerebral interference or sentiment. We do not have to reason what something is, and our preferential assessment is irrelevant in terms of direct cognition. Our quintessential singularity encounters the circumstance immediately and recognizes phenomena for their own intrinsic distinction. The concomitant knowledge that is discovered through immediate experience, by the essential identity of the human being, is the authentic condition of the phenomenon.

We experience a living phenomenon directly and recognize that it is a viable establishment of sequential, metamorphic intricacies whereby a cycle of development is achieved. All organisms are established, essentially alike in that they remain obedient to workable principles although they differ in nature according to the qualitative manner of their expression. The magnificence and ingenuity is scarcely comprehended through an analysis of the physical properties but the activity whereby the intricacies of arrangement are applied and arranged towards a specific end are readily recognizable through direct cognition.

To attribute living, functioning intricacies of arrangement to the caprice of inanimate influences not only defies logic it is revealed as absurd when the organic phenomenon is immediately recognized for what it really is through the direct engagement of the human quintessence.

The identification and application of a cognitive approach and practice that is immediate rather than oblique or abstract should be heralded as a break-through because phenomena are now directly engaged and intrinsically identified. It becomes possible at last to know what something is definitively. No longer need we reason as to its identity or construct theories and hypotheses and endlessly argue a preferred perspective. The human being has the inherent capacity to experientially know intrinsic identity and through the immediate engagement of the human essence, discover the essential identity of all other phenomena.

The artist and scientist, John Wilkes, published in 2003 what is undoubtedly a definitive work concerning the intrinsic, qualitative identity of water and the particular significance of its life bestowing capacity. Through a lifetime of research, experimentation and practical application, Wilkes diligently explored the inherent significance and distinctive nature of water. He revealed an essential dimension that goes far beyond our conventional understanding foundered merely upon a study of the physical properties. (Flowforms: The Rhythmic Power of Water by A. John Wilkes).

The remaining three Agencies have yet to be comprehensively explored for the vivifying qualities. Goethe's Theory of Colors examines the phenomenon of the colorful appearance of sunlight as it waxes and wanes. Numerous artists are well versed in the language of light and color but in comparison to the work of John Wilkes nothing similar has been approached for either air or warmth.

Yet, it is experientially familiar to most people that bubbling, fresh water from a mountain stream is invigorating both to touch and taste. A brisk ocean breeze is stimulating and golden sunlight upon the waves lifts the spirits, while the agreeable warmth of a summer's day produces contentment.

Conversely, to dwell near dull, sluggish waters encourages melancholy. Stale air produces stultification while Seasonal Affective Disorder is well known to many sufferers who crave the sunshine. Endless overcast skies provoke a disposition of dullness while debilitating cold or severe heat have obvious, adverse consequences.

The difference between the extremes lies in their quality. It is the qualitative dimension that is overlooked by the staunch materialist yet; quality is vitally significant and experientially blatant. It reveals the intrinsic yet intangible condition of a phenomenon. Water, revealed to be identical under physical analysis, is recognized as different depending upon its qualitative condition. This recognition may be similarly extended to all phenomena whereby a thoroughly more meaningful and expansive perspective towards life is achieved. An appreciation of the qualitative dimension offers profound and meaningful knowledge of the authentic condition of existence. This is far more meaningful intelligence than an exhaustive scrutiny of the physical appearance could ever achieve because it deals with the identities of phenomena, as they exist, in reality.

10. THE MATERIALISTIC WORLD-VIEW

Materialism is a severe impediment to the further development of human cognition. Remaining convinced of the exclusive authenticity of physical appearances and determined that only tangible evidence warrants consideration, we remain ignorant of a significant dimension of existence that is not merely physically founded. The neglected dimension is composed of the qualitative implications and distinctions that intrinsically identify phenomena.

If one were to assemble numerous birds eggs of different varieties and examine them for the minutiae of their diversity, it would quickly become evident that to exhaustively list their differences would require considerable scrutiny. Nevertheless, we would fail to arrive at a definitive identification, but we would have merely assembled a list of particulars.

However, examining the same bird's eggs for their qualitative distinctions, the first thing that strikes us is that they are all exactly the same in principle. That is to say, we recognize them all as bird's eggs through the commonalities that define them. Furthermore, while all bird eggs follow the same archetypal configuration, they differ individually through the qualitative expression of their particular distinction.

Similarly, a dozen acorns gathered from different oak trees all possess commonalities that identify them as acorns, but they are differentiated individually by the particular nature whereby the common basis is expressed. The qualitative distinction of the particular acorn is the same as that of the tree that bore it. An analysis of the acorn would reveal an exhaustive list of attributes, but that list would not resemble one garnered from a scrutiny of the tree of origin. In other words, physical properties do not identify the essential distinction that identifies a phenomenon.

Every phenomenon possesses a qualitative singularity that is its distinct identity. If the physical details and properties were scrupulously listed the resultant list would still remain remote from the essential existence. This is because physical properties are incommensurate with qualities. The intrinsic identity of a phenomenon is elusive because it is incorporeal. The appearance reveals something of the identity in terms of how it differs in a specific detail, but in order to articulate the essential distinction the phenomenon must be qualitatively identified. However, the qualitative distinction of a phenomenon is intangible and cannot be determined from an analysis of the physical conditions. Consequently, essential existence is discovered only through experiential cognition because it does not exist as a materially.

The dimension wherein qualities reside is inherent to the phenomenon and it is where the intrinsic distinction is found. It does not occur anywhere else in some hypothetical region of sensibility. It is the overlooked dimension of phenomenal existence that remains obscured through an exclusive obsession with the physical appearance.

An assertion of authentic knowledge is difficult to sustain when it cannot be physically examined nor adequately explored through reason. Thus, the materialistic approach remains for many, at first glance, the sole alternative because material properties can be analyzed, measured and, therefore, their authenticity is readily substantiated. Unfortunately, experientially justified, intangible values often remain excluded and, consequently, a cursory understanding of phenomena overlooks the more profound significances.

In other words, the exclusive material perspective, composed merely of physically, verifiable phenomena, is too limited. Furthermore, materialism, extrapolated as a philosophical doctrine is inadequate because much commonly experienced, intangible reality, remains excluded from consideration. Therefore, the dismissal of the qualitative dimension of existence, results in a conceptual reduction that is remote from experientially justified reality.

However, the difficulty with the religious as opposed to the material approach is that belief and faith in certain tenets, creeds or even revelation, cannot be definitively authenticated. In other words, apart from conviction, there is no reasonable way to determine

127

authenticity. Further, the follower, personally ignorant and having to accept a doctrinal outlook on trust, is subject to potential distortions of interpretation maintained as justified by the insistence of an elect authority. This has been exhaustively and insidiously demonstrated throughout history. The necessary reliance upon belief and faith, therefore, places the disciple in an extremely vulnerable position.

Yet similar to the faithful, who also abrogate their prerogative of cognitional autonomy to a more informed potency, the materialist cedes authority more to intellectual appraisal and not to fact. Frequently, there is much in the materialistic position that resembles faith and belief when a conviction is intensified by entrenched prejudice. Many claimants of superior, physically established knowledge are merely persuaded through the arguments of others and possess little authentic knowledge of their own discovery.

The approach whereby the determined materialist evaluates life is necessarily void of qualities because it relies exclusively upon the evidence of an analytical examination of physical properties. Yet, the human being cannot really deny values, qualities and intrinsic identities because it is known through common knowledge that they exist. The exclusively materialistic interpretation is, therefore, at odds with individual experience.

If the materialist, despite the blatant contradiction of personal experience with established, materialistic,

Western philosophy, allows that intangible significances may indeed deserve merit, even though they cannot be physically located, then the view of reality as existing exclusively of matter, is reduced to a fabrication. Thereby, there creeps into the barren mechanical, physical world-view of the materialist, the suspicion of a qualitative dimension to existence that cannot, in all integrity, be ignored.

Materialistic, Western philosophy is established upon the conviction that only physical phenomena possess definitive reality. Yet, to deny the existence of intangible qualities to material appearances is to remove everything of qualitative significance from human experience. But if the materialist begrudgingly cedes a tenuous reality to qualities then, all intangible values must be similarly acknowledged as probable and the conclusions of the former exclusive philosophy are thereby invalidated.

When the qualitative distinction of a thing is examined an entirely more poignant dimensional state of existence is revealed as the intrinsic condition of the blatant appearance. Indeed, it is the intangible, qualitative dissimilarities between material phenomena that, when directly engaged and recognized, present a glimpse of the authentic condition of existence.

For example, the essential quality of gold represented and described through the medium of poetry or any of the arts, is revealed to be of far greater significance that a purely material description would imply. For this reason, the intangible qualities that underlie physical evidence, intrinsically identify the phenomenon on the basis of substantive significance. In other words, every phenomenon possesses a qualitative distinction that reveals its authentic identity.

More precisely, the physical properties of phenomena do not represent the intrinsic identity, but they merely demonstrate an oblique perception of things. It is the qualitative distinction between phenomena that reveals their authentic significance; and it is the qualitative dimension, neglected and denied reality by materialistic, Western philosophy, that is recognized through direct experience, as the authentic condition of phenomena.

The intrinsic identity of something exists as the qualitative basis of expression that distinguishes it essentially from other phenomena. Of necessity, intrinsic distinction is ascertained only through immediate engagement because it is intangible, and consequently it can only be identified experientially. That is to say, qualities are experientially evident but otherwise elusive, but that does not imply nonexistence. Thus, we recognize that the intrinsic manner whereby something is expressed, is discovered not upon the scrutiny of the tangible details, but as the qualitative distinction of the entirety of its existence.

To put the matter another way, the intrinsic

distinction of something is a qualitatively expressive and consequently it is only discovered through the equally essential significance of the human being because whole, physically elusive identities require direct engagement in order to be determined. That is to say, profundity does not reside in the parts but only in the entirety.

It is whole identities that we wish to discover. We find that they exist as intrinsic significances that potentially possess physically independent existence. However, without the material carapace we would be unable to ascertain elusive significances because they would exist without physical conclusion, and we would be unable to find them. Nevertheless, phenomena possess intrinsic, elemental significance that is entirely extant and immediately apparent from the perspective of the similarly essential individual human ipseity.

Be that as it may, the intangible significance of something does not reside in a separate and mysterious realm, but more moderately, it exists as an overlooked dimension of what is otherwise already physically apparent. Consequently, when the qualitative significances of phenomena are recognized through direct engagement, we become cognizant of the existence of a layer of additional complexity. Therefore, we are not suggesting that there exists an ephemeral counterpart or a conflicting realm; we are merely engaging that which is already known, more profoundly for the intrinsic significance that meaningfully underlies the superficial appearance.

Recognition of the profound significance of a phenomenon is achieved through an immediate experience of its original condition. The original condition of the object is determined directly, whereas conventionally, our interpretation and preconceptions concerning it would have predominated. However, when the human, essential singularity is established as our principal and elemental existence, the sovereign existence of the human being engages things immediately.

In order to directly engage circumstances from the perspective of the human, essential ipseity, the familiar practices of preconception, association and partiality must be restrained. Thereby, of necessity, the perspective of the ipseity prevails.

However, the obvious discrepancy between an exclusively materialistic theory and experientially achieved knowledge concerning existence is conveniently dismissed by marginalizing essential and qualitative intelligence as merely subjective or anecdotal. Furthermore, the conviction that physical appearances exclusively embody the significance of phenomena hinders the original approach. Indeed, it is very hard for the materialist to grasp that there exists a profounder volume that is of greater significance than the material appearance because the materialist finds tangible evidence reassuring, and definitive.

Regrettably, an abstract simplification of existence

has become established that is at odds with even ordinary experience. For example, the materialist steadfastly insists that factory farm produce, that is force grown on artificial fertilizers under unnatural conditions, is identical to organically raised vegetables. Yet, conversely, the same advocate contradicts the former position when a difference in taste and smell between two, otherwise physically identical vegetables, is acknowledged to their advantage. In the same way, the qualitative difference between wine vintages is ignored through a physical analysis that reveals them to be identically composed. Yet, their distinctions are poetically described and authenticated by the experienced palate of the sommelier.

The abstract materialist philosopher presents a contrived perspective towards life that reduces everything into tangible terms at the expense of the profound. Yet, the philosophical construct is applied only selectively. Describing an excellent vintage wine, clearly a chemical analysis is inadequate and even the staunchest materialist readily applies the artistic medium of poetry in order to express the qualities and virtues of a favorite claret. Indeed, there are forty agreed ways to describe the quality of a vintage while only one of them references a physical property: acidity. Qualitative distinctions such as these while authentic and real, cannot be justified through analysis or described in technical terms. Yet, they are real albeit incorporeal, qualities and, as every sommelier knows, they definitively identify the particular wine.

But qualitative realities are flatly denied significant existence when it is respectfully suggested that they indicate a more significant dimension of existence. What was formerly an impressive evaluation of the identity of a fine vintage wine is reduced to merely the amusing pleasantry of the sommelier. But anything that may even remotely concede reasonable ground to the possibility of significant incorporeal existence is explained away or summarily dismissed.

This strange contradiction is the result of an excessive reliance upon abstract rational at the expense of intelligence attained through immediate experience. Experiential knowledge is easily denied existence if it even remotely challenges the entrenched conviction that the material appearance is the only significant reality. One cannot help thinking that the determined maintenance of a contrived doctrine is imagined to be of greater significance than ingenuous research.

Yet, everything can be examined and compared for its qualitative intrinsicality. The distinction between two objects does not rest exclusively upon their physical properties. Indeed, phenomena very similar in appearance may be qualitatively remote. Thereby, through immediate cognition, we discover that the qualitative distinctions between material appearances possess intrinsic significance and reveal their authentic identities upon the basis of their essential expression.

In other words, qualitative distinctions are recognized, through immediate, experiential cognition, to be the authentic identity of phenomena. That is, intrinsic distinction is discovered when phenomena are engaged in their condition of original existence by the human essence. It is this qualitative identity that substantively differentiates one object from another and distinguishes between two similar, phenomenal appearances. Thus, the identification of the qualitative identity of a thing far surpasses the mere, superficial appearance. Yet, the significance remains entirely intangible. Thus, it is recognized that a vastly meaningful, essential component of existence is overlooked by the materialistic approach, while its identification, through immediate experience, restores vitality, significance and dimension to a banal interpretation of existence.

Every human being is inherently able to directly experience the qualitative intrinsicality of things by virtue of our individual essential existence. Exasperatingly, the contrived, materialistic perspective contradicts both incorporeal human significance and the value of intelligence achieved through immediate engagement. This would matter less, but it has become a severely entrenched position that undermines straightforward understanding. That is to say, life has become a riddle not because it is inevitably mysterious, but through misinterpretation.

Consequently, phenomena continue to be identified merely by their superficial appearances. And a materialistically established, abstract artifice contradicts what we know of existence through immediate engagement. Nevertheless, the significance of a phenomena lies not in the physical but, most impressively, with its essential qualitative existence. Thus, the qualitative singularity of a phenomenon, engaged in the condition of its original existence, represents the more profound aspect of its identity.

Observing two rocks, one igneous and the other crystalline, direct cognition, avoiding abstract rationalism or aesthetic preference, enters a condition of immediate experience and engages the phenomena originally. Direct apprehension inaugurates a straightforward encounter between our own significant existence and the essential identity of the phenomenon. Thereby, through cognitive immediacy the samples are recognized as they exist essentially and the qualitative distinctions that differentiate them are instantly apparent.

Our two samples are recognized for their qualitative singularity, which is indicative of the intrinsic, qualitative distinction. At no point do we refer to their physical properties, but nevertheless, we establish a concise representation of their natures. Although, conventionally they are solely classified according to their material metrics and blatant appearances, seldom are they intrinsically distinguished through immediate cognition, upon the basis of the intangible significances.

Direct cognition, because it is immediate and deals with an instant engagement between the essential existence of the human being and the inherence of the phenomenon, determines the authentic identity. It experiences things as they are, immediately. Thus, two different natures of mineral are directly experienced and known for their qualitative distinctions instead of being classified, merely according to the results of an analysis of their obvious properties and appearances.

Therefore, through immediate engagement, the discovery of qualitative intrinsically, as the authentic identity that distinguishes one mineral from another, is recognized as an inherent, human capacity. Consequently, direct cognition through the human, essential identity reveals the authentic distinction of every other phenomenon. This is because the nature of intrinsic, phenomenal identity is intransient and incorporeal; whereupon the otherwise elusive, essential identity is cognitively compatible and qualitatively commensurate with the human quintessence.

Further, the comparison between an acorn for its qualitative nature, and a rock reveals immediately that the one is organic and while the other is inert. They are of a vastly different nature from one another. They each possess a qualitative singularity that distinguishes them from similar representatives of their respective kingdoms, but, through direct apprehension, we recognize the qualitative remoteness between the mineral and vegetable realms. We recognize that they are essentially unalike and the notion that organic life arose spontaneously from the mineral kingdom is entirely dismissed through an intimate understanding of essential incompatibility.

But two different varieties of acorn compared side by side reveal both qualitative distinction and essential similarities. What distinguishes the two is the manner in which a common ideal is differently interpreted. They are differentiated by the intrinsic qualities while each is also a variation upon a certain, more general conceptualization. The commonality shared by both is archetypal, revealed in this instant as the acorn appearance, according to which each variety, essentially conforms.

The one rock is qualitatively distinct from another yet, both remain mineral rocks. The acorns are identified for their differences of expression, yet both are recognized as biological acorns. Yet, they belong each to specific domains that are similarly qualitatively distinct.

Furthermore, one is able to recognize incorporeal realities as unequivocally extant and upon this knowledge a sense for profundity is established that is not confined to material appearances and physical properties nor founded upon an abstract typology.

Direct experience of intangible significances enables the human being to steadily develop an autonomy of cognition whereby abstraction is replaced with a direct, personal engagement of the incorporeal dimension of existence.

This is a necessary advancement from the myopic, materialistic perspective and, steadily, a considerable foundation of experientially acknowledged, incorporeal significance is established. But the immediate engagement of phenomena in the condition of their original and essential existence involves not intellectual abstraction but immediacy. Thereupon, human theories may be tried and evaluated for their fundamental soundness or contradicted from the perspective of an intimate knowledge of immediately engaged profundity, and determined for their significance through qualitative comparison.

Similarly, through immediate experience the fundamental concept of the human being is elevated from a materialistically founded definition wherein only the superficial is recognized. Thus, instead of the distorted condemnation of people as soulless, biological automata, direct, experiential cognition reveals the human, essential singularity to be of significant independent existence. Thereby, the distinction between two people no longer rests upon their outward appearances but is discovered to be both essential and intransient.

METAPHORIC AND FIGURATIVE TERMS USED TO DESCRIBE THE QUALITIES OF WINE

ACIDITY ... ANGULAR ... AUSTERE ... BARNYARD ...

BIG ... BRIGHT ... BUTTERY ... CASSIS ... CHARCOAL ...

CHEWY TANNINS ... CIGAR BOX ... COMPLEX ...

CREAMY ... CRISP ... DENSE ... EARTHY ... ELEGANT ...

FAT ... FLABBY ... FLAMBOYANT ... FLESHY ...

FOOD FRIENDLY ... GRIPPY ... HINT OF ...

INTELLECTUALLY SATISFYING ... JAMMY ... JUICY ...

LASER-LIKE ... LEES ... MINERALLY ... OAKED ...

OPULENT ... REFINED ... SILKY ... STEELY ...

STRUCTURED ... TIGHT ... TOASTY ... UNCTUOUS ...

UNOAKED ... VELVETY

11. INTRINSIC QUALITATIVE IDENTIFICATION

The significance of the discrepancy between physical appearances and intrinsic existence is further emphasized when it is realized that both manners of depiction assume possession of the authentic identity of a phenomenon. The exclusive examination of material properties is the foundation upon which conventional characterization is established, while the discovery of intangible, qualitative significances presents an entirely different portrayal. While both perspectives possess merit, the physical appearance is recognized as only superficial compared to the essential condition.

The miss-assumption that blatant, physical properties alone serve as the entirety of a phenomenon is further exacerbated by abstract dialectic. Abstract rationalism is applied in an attempt to qualify a shallow perspective that is otherwise recognized through immediate engagement as untenable. Consequently, a contrived, intellectual position is maintained as if it somehow represented the reality more effectively than direct experience.

Abandoning an interpretation of life according to a preconceived structure, by means of which we imagine that we can understand existence, instead we engage circumstances originally. Therefore, through directness, the intrinsic identity of phenomena are discovered to the degree that mental and emotional evaluation are restrained. Thereby, it is found that the human being also possesses intrinsic singularity and we are subsequently able to engage other situations from the perspective of our own essential existence. In other words, when we curb the intrusive, reasoning faculty and we attend to circumstances immediately we discern the profundity of things. Formerly we understood phenomena obliquely through our established preconceptions, corroborated by abstract reason. However, when a phenomenon is engaged by the human, intrinsic identity, direct apprehension reveals the meaningful identification.

It matters little how we imagine existence to be or how we reasonably qualify our convictions. Reality exists as an extant condition that must be directly experienced by the human essence in order to be recognized. Otherwise, we entertain only a contrived understanding that is typically remote from certitude.

Indeed, it is unrealistic to intellectually estimate the authenticity of an existential interpretation because reason calculates, but it cannot discern. Further, the fact that real or unreal cannot be quantified reveals the inadequacy of an exclusively intellectual interpretation towards existence. Rationalism only ever effectively deals with those things that can be deliberated, and the further the consideration is from calculable quantities the more tenuous the conclusion.

However, through direct observation a knowledge of the qualitative significances of a phenomenon becomes discernible. That is to say, when the human, essential identity immediately experiences something the encounter occurs within the condition of reality by virtue of the directness of the engagement. Accordingly, abstract evaluation even when it is considered objectively informed by the proponent, is recognized as oblique when compared to the immediate, experiential approach because it is necessarily discursive. That is why immediate, experiential cognition provides direct knowledge concerning the nature of existence while rational deduction will always remain polemical.

An attempted identification of a phenomenon exclusively through the examination of its obvious appearance is simplistic and contrived. It is contrived in the sense that considerably more of the intrinsic nature of what something is can be experientially known, but identity remain elusive through an investigation solely of the material structure. Indeed, a material scrutiny is more likely to concern the workings of something than the integral significance.

However, in terms of a predominantly materially derived understanding of existence, the obvious appearance takes precedence. Paradoxically, the materialist will deny material exclusivity but require that all evidence should correspond with physical metrics in order to be justified. In other words, materialistic exclusivity inevitably excludes all information except that which is derived from matter. Consequently, the generally most predominant philosophy of our time is established upon the obvious condition of things and not the profound.

In other words, it is imagined, that to assess an object merely upon the strength of the most easily evidenced properties, is bound to be the reliable approach to understanding. However, we consider that perspective only ostensibly justified because it applies exclusively to the obvious. Consequently, the intangible significance of a thing, recognized experientially, is conventionally deemed less significant than the physical carapace and readily discarded as ephemeral by the materialist. However, the requirement of physical justification is legitimate if we do not recognize the existence of a more profound magnitude that the most conspicuous manifestation.

Nevertheless, we cannot simply disregard essential significances as if they did not exist, because plainly they do. For example, if we consider one another merely biological, inevitably, the narrowness of our view bodes very badly for meaningful human relationships. Similarly, if we cannot discern between profundity and superficiality because we deny the existence of intangible merit, we will be unable to determine between cultural progression and regression.

Unfortunately a materialistic ascendancy has become an entrenched perspective. Therefore, a pre-established mindset prevents a straightforward openminded inquiry. But we know full well that ourselves and other people are more significant than the corporeal aspect, and that culture elevates the human soul through the intrinsic significance of a particular artistic medium. And what we are endeavoring to describe is the approach whereby profundity may be objectively ascertained and identified.

The dogmatic resistance against critical metaphysical inquiry has arisen because of a long and dubious, historical admixture of belief, superstition and mysticism, that remains to this day the foundation of many incoherent ideologies. Furthermore, an innocent mind is readily convinced by premeditated persuasiveness and collective pressure including the desire of association. But openminded research does not intentionally promote an ideology. Indeed, the opposite is true. If, through the immediate engagement of material conditions, the observer seeks a greater profundity than merely the obvious, to the degree that the familiar cognitive faculties are restrained, the essential significance of phenomena becomes evident.

Granting credence to the existence of the intrinsic significance of a material phenomenon offers the perceptive observer a glimpse of an entirely overlooked dimension to existence. The recognition of the qualitative expression of an entity, for example, reveals the error of allowing an abstractly conceived philosophy to establish an interpretative, materialistic filter through which existence is evaluated. Thereby, the intrinsic identification of things is entirely overlooked. Needless to say, the primary obstacle preventing the observer from an immediate experience of qualitative dimensionality is the prejudice of a preconceived interpretation.

Physical properties are easy to assess and through quantification, they are readily managed and manipulated in the abstract through computer simulation or even virtual reality. Indeed, laboratories are often full of machinery because technologies most readily represent and further elaborate quantified data. Therefore, by ease of assessment the apparent totality of things are thought to offer definitive evidence as to the identity of the entire phenomenon. In reality, they merely offer evidence concerning the calculable properties of the physical appearance and fail to approach the essential existence.

The intangible qualities of a phenomenon cannot be assessed and evaluated abstractly. They defy measurement and calculation and the intellect can do little with them but speculate. It is, therefore, hardly surprising that a mind that is abstractly preoccupied and convinced of the exclusive significance of the material appearance as the sole reality of a phenomenon, should fail to recognize that which cannot be physically discerned. Furthermore, the materialist is content to remain with conventional associations and preconceptions, delving no further than the superficial appearance. This position is exacerbated by the fundamental ignorance of the materialist concerning the existence of intangible identity which is unrecognizable through the prevailing materialistic orthodoxy. In fact, the very suggestion that appearances belie an intrinsic, qualitative existence remains unpalatable to the preoccupied materialist.

Yet, an obvious contradiction remains between the recognition of the existence of qualities through experience, and the artifice of a materialistic position that is established beforehand as exclusively justified. Original engagement, without allegiance to a pre-conceptual position, must surely be the ultimate aspiration of the sincere and deliberate, empirical researcher.

The materialist wishes to delve no further and is content to cease experiential cognition while remaining preoccupied with an indirect and abstract evaluation of existence.But, oblique assessment compounds an already prejudiced perspective with further intellectual abstraction.

The assessment of exclusively physically derived information is a very remote and obscure practice compared with knowledge directly attained through experiential cognition. Phenomena, directly engaged are discovered to possess qualitative significances; and there is no retreat from the caliber of intelligence, immediately achieved, into previously established prejudice. Nevertheless, the qualitative dimension of phenomenal appearances is only abstractly disputed because of the elaborate extension of the idea of physical exclusivity. Experientially, intrinsic existence is thoroughly justified.

The abstractly preoccupied thinker will maintain that intangible significances are imagined while simultaneously evaluating phenomena introspectively and indirectly, unaware of a contradiction. This extraordinary inconsistency reveals the vulnerable nature of a prejudicial intellectual approach. Further, when confronted with qualitative essentials that are clearly authentic but can only be described metaphorically or figuratively, the materialist becomes selective. Some qualities must be begrudgingly accepted because to deny them is paramount to insanity. But other directly known, incorporeal significances are discarded altogether.

However, the most significant harm rests upon the determination to ignore the implications and ramifications of the acceptance of significant intangible existence. The materialist understands full well that once the authenticity of a chosen few intangible values is ceded then the intrinsic merit of all qualities must be similarly recognized as plausible.

Be that as it may, the direct, experiential examination of an object for its qualitative value and expression reveals an intrinsic nature founded upon essential significance. Furthermore, the intrinsic disposition is not merely an adjunct qualification of the physical but it is the authentic identity. This is discovered solely through experiential engagement and remains elusive to the exclusively materialistic perspective. But, of greater importance, the materialist need not be concerned about a descent into vague religiosity and unsubstantiated make-believe because the approach concerns not faith but immediate cognition.

Regrettably, the establishment of an abstract contrivance founded upon the oblique, intellectual consideration of the physical as a satisfactory substitute for experientially derived and known intelligence, leads to lamentable consequences. Thereby, the world remains unknown to us as it in fact is, but it is replaced by an exclusive, material counterfeit that is predominantly superficial. Indeed, the possible repercussions of the comprehensive denial of the existence of a meaningful qualifying volume to existence blocks access to a deeper understanding. This is one of the reasons why many flock to frequently questionable doctrinal affiliation. If the fundamental concept of immediate cognition is entirely dismissed then serious research towards substantive existence loses intelligent direction.

Through exclusive attention to abstract evaluation and intellectual interpretation, the essential identity of a phenomenon is lost and remains indeterminable, concealed by the dogged insistence of a solely materialistic perspective towards existence. However, cerebral thinking does not have the capacity to evaluate and assess intangible qualities. But, having ceded exclusive, cognitive authority to the power of the intellect, direct cognition remains unexplored.

Direct cognition requires the immediate engagement of the human, intrinsic singularity with the phenomenon in order to experience circumstances in a condition of absolute, existential integrity. The materialist is predictably convinced that human identity is corporeally established. Hence, direct cognition, if ceded any value at all by the skeptic, is regarded merely as a practice of heightened observation.

However, the significance of an immediate encounter between the human essence and the physical appearance of an object, whereby the intrinsic identity is discovered, is that both the human essence and the intrinsic identity of the phenomenon are of an alike intrinsic significance. Therefore, it is through the immediacy of the engagement between the human essence and the essential identity of the object that knowledge concerning incorporeal existence is achieved.

In summary, the abstractly envisioned, materialistic world-view is a deceptive, cognitive perspective because of the remote and oblique manner of its conception. Adopting a philosophy that interprets life exclusively upon the basis of physical appearances, while ignoring the intrinsic value and qualities of phenomena, is an extraordinarily superficial conceit. But it is less a failure to recognize the significant existence of intrinsic qualities and values that is at fault, but rather, their indifferent dismissal.

Material exclusivity is expounded through the intellectual re-ordering of physical data and their consequent, distorted, disingenuous evaluation reduces existence to a capricious inter-reaction of anonymous material and random forces. Exclusively founded upon physical properties the results of materialistic, Western philosophy offer a predictably barren interpretation of life remote from reality.

Nevertheless, the experiential exploration of essential, qualitative significances as the intrinsic identity of phenomena, reveals existence to be vastly more meaningful and estimable than that suggested by the contrived perspective of materialism. The significance of a direct recognition of qualitative distinctions is further compounded by the fact that they are pragmatically recognized as real through the immediate engagement of the experientially authenticated essence of the human being. Furthermore, unavoidably we directly experience qualities and nuances of value throughout everyday life. But we do not cede the same significance to qualities as we do to physical appearances because we do not understand what the intrinsic, qualitative differentiation of a phenomenon is.

However, by dismissing value as something of intrinsic significance, we are scarcely aware that the human, essential identity resides in the midsts of intangible, qualitatively distinct, realities. Thus, we only vaguely recognize the immanence of an incorporeal dimension to existence because we have become convinced that our own direct knowledge of the qualitative somehow pales in comparison to the authoritative edicts of materialistic, Western philosophy.

In other words, we have granted a monopoly of understanding to the meager and superficial perspective of the materialist. In all likelihood, this insufficient position is founded more upon the conviction of the exclusive significance of the physical appearance, intensified by abstract rationalism concerning it, rather than deceit. Nevertheless, it is the obligation of every individual who desires cognitive autonomy to strive and directly apprehend existence in a manner untainted by the prejudice of convention.

Otherwise, phenomena that usually are solely identified on the strength of their material appearances and through tangible evidence gleaned from an analysis of their physical properties, lamentably, seem the full extent of existence.

The difference between the physical appearance and the qualitative distinction of things is immediately discernible through comparison. For example, the recognition of the quality of one variety of oak compared to another is of a singularly greater dimension than merely the comparison of the appearance of their parts.

Similarly, the lumber of the walnut tree examined side by side with that of the oak is recognized as qualitatively distinct. A somatic analysis of the two reveals different physical and chemical properties but upon that basis alone, the identity of the essential distinction between them remains remote. While the superficial properties, chemical composition, hardness and stress value are of use to the engineer they do not tell little concerning the essential significances.

Nevertheless, both wood samples possess a unique quality of warmth and depth of beauty even though the qualitative distinctions cannot be calibrated by degree. That is to say, the exotic nature of a wood cannot be physically isolated in the way of the material aspects and tangible properties. Indeed, delight to the eye and subtlety of figuration are unrevealed through physics, mathematical calculation or mechanics.

Nevertheless, qualitative value is absolutely real and of profound significance as every experienced wood artisan intimately knows. In a similar manner, the raven and the dove are birds of distinctly different appearance. Again, the disparities and form semblances may be exhaustively scrutinized, measured and tabulated according to their physical condition. While both retain the avian commonality, the distinction between them is less founded upon their material aspects but rather established upon the qualitative manner in which they express themselves through the common avian principle. Thereby, the singular distinction of each is recognized as a difference of intrinsic identity and not merely extrinsic, physical appearance.

155

It is the singular intrinsic identity that we wish to ascertain because thereby the authentic particularity of a phenomenon is revealed. Nevertheless, the observant ornithologist naturally recognizes distinctions of character between birds but even so does not establish classification upon the basis of intrinsic identity.

In other words, we are suggesting that the appearances of phenomena are insufficient indicators of identification and that the neglected intrinsicality reveals a vastly more profound dimension to existence than does mere apparency. Predictably, the argument will be eagerly proffered by the materialist that qualitative and merely subjective distinctions differ according to the predilection of the particular observer. Indeed, if our cognitive capacity were solely limited to abstract rationalism concerning material appearances then the protestation of subjectivity would be valid.

But the human being has a hitherto underdeveloped ability that arises from the manner whereby our own intrinsicality of being engages a phenomenon immediately. Thereby, the qualitative distinctions between two similar phenomena, through direct apprehension, are recognized not through preferential evaluation but immediately, as the inherent significance that comprises the intrinsic identity. Therefore, we restrain both our dialectic rationalism and our conventional subjectivity when we engage a phenomenon directly from the perspective of our own quintessence. Indeed, it is essential we do so in order that the singular, qualitative significances of phenomena may be revealed as they are in reality and not merely, prejudicially evaluated.

Through this exposition we recognize by comparison the shortcomings of a materialistic philosophy that concedes reality solely to physical appearances. Yet, the superficial interpretation of phenomena is staunchly maintained and qualified through abstract argument even in the face of individual experience to the contrary.

Abstraction is beguiling because of the sequential manner whereby we expound upon a position, while logic seems alike in structure to mathematics and similarly convincing. However, existence does not consist of solely quantifiable properties but also of qualities that mathematics and logical reasoning are powerless to evaluate. Therefore, attention to the intangible value of an object reveals the significance of the intrinsic identity that is more significance than the appearance.

Immediate, experiential cognition through the human, essential identity demonstrates that the exclusively materialistic perspective towards life is a superficial approach that fails in practice. Above all, the human being craves meaningfulness and substantive understanding but it is not found upon a merely shallow examination of things nor through abstract conjecture. However, through immediate cognition, the individual essence of the human being is ables to independently discern the significant volume of existence of things and impressive deepen individual understanding.

12. DIRECT EXPERIENTIAL COGNITION

The essential distinction between phenomena exists as the intangible, yet intrinsic, qualitative significance. But essential qualities cannot be expressed in the same manner as physical properties because of their incorporeal nature. However, convention requires that phenomena be described by their appearances even though intrinsic significances are not materially represented, and the physical appearance belies the essential identity. Qualitative distinctions are the intangible, intrinsic significances that distinguish phenomena beyond their common properties. Therefore, the means whereby impalpable distinctions and identities are communicated is necessarily artistic and metaphoric because they exist intangibly.

There are forty, accepted and elaborate metaphoric and figurative terms used by the skilled sommelier to communicate the qualitative distinction between different wines. Indeed, a wine is more successfully distinguished through its quality than by its physical properties. Consequently, experiential knowledge reveals the existence of very distinct natures that are known to be authentic yet, they cannot be physically justified.

Based upon experientially known singularities, the intrinsic, yet intangible identity of a wine in terms of taste, is more precisely discerned with greater experience.

Wines are usually differentiated through their qualitative significances, and a physical analysis would only represent the uni-dimensionally. Indeed, an exhaustive reduction of the material itself may even reveal two very distinct vintages as identical. Predictably, any dissimilarities that are determined through material analysis pale compared to the poetic representation of the sommelier.

This comparison is not merely used as a parallel to reveal the shortcomings of a materialistic representation of the world but it is precisely the manner whereby a superficial perspective, founded only upon physical properties, replaces that which is known to be directly, significantly, and of course, experientially valid. Thereby, the qualitative merit of phenomena is discounted in preference to physical considerations. Consequently, an examination of the physical properties alone falls short of immediately determined experiential knowledge. The quality of the woods we depicted when engaging them directly and experientially in the previous chapter does not appear in a material analysis because physically illusive essentials have to be immediately encountered in order to be known.

Similarly, if assorted acorn varieties are analyzed, they are discovered to be virtually undifferentiated. Yet, in terms of form-emphasis and character, they are recognized as qualitatively, very distinct. By logical extension, compounded through experiential cognition, the human identity is similarly recognized as far more significant than our blatant physical appearance. In fact, the distinction between human beings lies less in the appearance and vastly more significantly, with the intrinsic distinction of our singularity.

In other words, the recognition of an alternative, yet valid, qualitative identity pertaining to phenomena reveals an authentic, intrinsic dimension to existence, beyond the superficial appearance.

Thus, the quality and identity of the wine described poetically by the sommelier is justified and readily acceptable by experiential consensus. Yet, when it is proposed that all phenomena possess a similarly intangible distinction and a significant, qualitative identity whereby they may be distinguished, the materialist strongly objects. The physical appearance is once again declared to be the sole reality.

The distinctions of intangible, qualitative significances intrinsic to phenomena identify them with far greater profundity than a depiction of the physical appearance. Sadly, a defensive retort to the contrary is all that may be expected in response to this statement because the existence of intangible significances is only vindicated through experiential cognition. They cannot be materially verified or qualified through abstractly argued rationalism.

Imagining for an instant, the world, inclusive of ourselves, as consisting of intrinsic qualities, subtleties of value and essential identities, and we recognize existence more profoundly. That is to say, the dimensionality revealed upon an examination of the essential, qualitative distinctions between phenomena, and recognized through an immediate apprehension of the intrinsic singularity, is entirely more significant than our conventional, superficial perspective.

Materialistic Western philosophy is an impoverished and entrenched mentality. It is a stubborn, contrived position that refuses to follow simple yet logical reasoning that may show the existence of a far more meaningful reality and, further, it denies the cognitive significance of a direct experience of qualitative distinctions. So it seems remarkably superficial that the physicality of phenomena is elevated as solely valid, while the qualitative distinctions are marginalized and condemned as subjective. Incredulously, it is asserted that phenomenal identity is composed only of the physical appearance and nothing else is deemed of comparable significance. Ironically, the essential existence of the materialist is self-condemned to similar insignificance.

Increasingly existence has become defined by material appearances. Subtleties of value, qualities and characteristic distinctions are largely discounted. Therefore, established upon the superficial, a meaningless counterfeit of reality has insinuated itself upon the human mentality. The superficial view is upheld through an extrapolation of information derived solely from physical appearances, with abstract ramifications that are, inevitably, of the same materialistic nature. In like manner, qualities, while permitted marginal existence only with a certain condescension, are not seriously included in the materialistic world-view and cannot challenge physical exclusivity. Not surprisingly, intangible, qualitative evidence is reduced to the realm of whimsy and derided as quaint.

The insidious manner whereby this distorted, exclusively materialistic perspective has monopolized the human outlook is further compounded when it is realized that the materialist applies this deception universally.

Thus, through the relentlessness of an over-reached, pseudo-science it is clear that the world, inclusive of the human being has been conceptually reduced to its physical rudiments. In that case, a conviction exists that we are the product of material law and operate exclusively under physical principles. Indeed, the materialist will claim that we are entirely the product of physical circumstances, and that which has been discovered of the laws only concerning matter, suffices to account for organic life and human significance.

Leaving the materialist behind to a restricted and myopic perspective and to the plight of closed-mindedness and prejudice, we continue with our exploration of a reality of vastly greater significance than the superficial, physical appearance. We replace abstract conceptualization with direct cognition, engage the human, intrinsic singularity and discover the essential identity of one another and the authentic existence of things. We approach them immediately and experientially recognize them for their qualitative significance.

Thereby, the human being is correctly reestablished as individually unique and the world is resurrected from the grip of lifeless forces that the materialist determinedly maintains produce organic organization. Furthermore, those intangible qualities are recognized as indicators of intrinsic significance because they are descriptive of the manner of the existence of things. Consequently, it is immediately evident through immediate cognition that qualitative, intangible distinctions are of far greater substance than the appearance and that a vast incorporeal world of enormous consequence is accessible because of the human, innate faculty of straightforward engagement.

The forty metaphors mentioned above, used to describe a fine wine, merely serve as an example of that which exists but cannot be defined in physical terms or discovered through chemical analysis. That which is revealed to the refined palette of the sommelier is communicated poetically because physically explicit terminology falls short. Yet, it is merely the taste and the bouquet that is being painstakingly identified and figuratively articulated. The color of the liquid itself may require an additional forty terms in order to express experiential knowledge to another human being. Yet, all these intrinsic qualities exist as authentic distinctions that identify the essential nature of phenomenal existence.

If we extend and apply this consideration to all phenomena, including the human being, it becomes self-evident that to know a thing for its authenticity, an entirely different cognitive approach is more necessary than that with which we are conventionally familiar. Immediate, experientially achieved knowledge of the intrinsic is discovered through direct cognition by the human, essential identity. Qualities cannot be reasoned or described in physical terms because they are intangible. Being incorporeal, the language of art is required in order to communicate the nature of their identities. Further, it is clear that an entirely different perspective towards existence emerges through the practice of direct cognition that is neither remote nor ephemeral. Thus, it becomes self-evident that we dwell amid a condition established upon an incorporeal significance of incredible richness.

While the language for communicating intangible realities may be poetry or any other exacting, artistic medium, the manner of knowing the authentic essence of a phenomenon is direct, experiential cognition. Everything can be known for its qualitative identity. Just as the sommelier isolates and identifies the qualities of a fine vintage, every human being has the similar capacity to discover for themselves the authentic identity of a phenomenon.

The parallel to the skill of the sommelier is used here merely to argue for the authenticity of intangible realities. Those opposed to this approach will determinedly counter and argue away the existence of qualitative essentials to naught. That is to say, rationale is subjectively applied in this manner towards the denial of the qualitatively intangible which is otherwise directly experienced as authentic.

In the same vein, the human intellect works most effectively when dealing with quantities, ideally when somehow phenomena can be mathematically assessed. Failing this, cerebral thinking attempts to analyze imponderables in a piece-meal fashion, imagining that the entirety may be understood through a scrutiny of the details. However, this is an entirely abstract approach because the identity of the whole does not exist in the parts. Therefore, reduction and logically sequential argument toward the identification of an object are an intellectually contrived approach that in reality is insufficient because it does not reveal the authentic existence. In other words, reduction examines the properties of the parts which possess a different distinction when isolated from the whole. Thereby, an artificial approach is established that replaces reality with a perspective that is figured-out and where the emphasis, of necessity, rests upon physical properties. Clearly, the materialistic perspective deals exclusively with tangible evidence to the detriment of all other considerations, and through analysis reduces phenomena not to parts of the same, but to different entities.

However, an incorporeal distinction, that despite its intangible existence, is recognized and authenticated as extant through common consensus, nonetheless, cannot be included in a materially exclusive evaluation of existence unless it can be quantified. But the only aspects of a phenomenon that can be reduced to numeric value are either already physical, or they are those that can be manipulated to seem as if they are quantifiable, while apparently remaining authentic to their original condition.

This conceals a slight-of-hand. The quantifiable attributes of a phenomenon do not represent the intrinsic identity. They will always remain, simply, further superficial evidence. In other words, quantities are merely the isolated aspects from the entirety that can be manipulated to seem as if the whole is numerically reducible.

This may be illustrated through an exploration of the qualitative existence of the color yellow. Yellow, in its ideal condition, possesses an intrinsic identity that distinguishes it from other colors. The master painter uses yellow, fully aware of its intrinsic identity, with purposeful skill in order that a painting may entirely describe a certain, otherwise discreet content. Therefore, the qualitative nature of the color yellow is expertly used to achieve a very specific communication.

However, materialistic Western philosophy does not acknowledge an intrinsic existence to qualitative significances. Indeed, the abstract rationalist manages physical appearances very well because rationalism can justify and authenticate material things on the strength of their tangible properties. For example, yellow is reduced to a measurable wavelength whose numerical value is asserted as its authentic identity. Colors, as the properties of sunlight are similarly deemed to be without intrinsic and autonomous significance. But the qualitative existence of yellow is not revealed through numerical symbology but only through immediate experience. That is, quantification is only possible if a phenomenal property is quantifiable. But the entirety of a phenomenon is not limited to its quantifiable aspects. Indeed, it is safe to say that nothing is without physically elusive qualification. Consequently, numerical substitution remains remote from the authentic condition of the phenomenon and only the most obdurate and dogmatic materialist would maintain otherwise.

The moment a phenomenon is directly experienced in present timing by the human, essential singularity and the activity of association with prior conceptualizations is restrained, the authenticity of intangible, essential identities becomes known. To the degree busy, abstract, cerebral activity is postponed, and a thing is encountered immediately, it is recognized for its intrinsic existence and not merely by its appearance. Thus, through the immediate engagement of phenomena by the human essence, qualitative distinctions become directly apparent. They are discovered extant, in an immanently experienced condition, revealing a dimension of existence far richer and more extensive than one composed solely of   physical   appearances   and   their properties.

13. THE SIGNIFICANCE OF DIRECT COGNITION

Returning to basics, we examine what is definitively known. It is recognized, as before, that the fullest extent of cognition that can be reached conventionally cannot approach that which is discovered through immediate, experiential engagement. For example, the human ipseity remains elusive to an examination of physical properties or through the rational evaluation of transient appearances. But the conventional, materialistic approach would have us believe that the superficial semblance comprises the full extent of our existence. We remain, consequently, only cognizant of the peripheral condition and we extend this frugal perspective, through our abstract manner of evaluation, to comprise the entirety. Yet, we know experientially, without the help of the intellect, that the human, essential identity is both extant and significant, and further, that it exists incorporeally.

Immediate engagement through the human, essential existence solves cognitive limitation. In other words, it is helpful to recognize that cerebral evaluation is necessarily limited to a very specific nature of information, operating indirectly through reason and functioning abstractly, after the cognitive event has passed. Additionally, endeavoring to establish what something is through sentimental evaluation is similarly flawed because neither approach offers definitive knowledge of the essential distinction of things.

The mystical approach towards life is similarly unsatisfactory. While the human essence may be experienced directly, the ascetic cares nothing for the phenomenal world. Thus, the incorporeal essential of the human constitution remains introverted and cannot achieve cognitive objectivity. Therefore, oblivious to the significance that underlies the physical appearance of nature, the mystic imagines the world to be entirely illusory.

Furthermore, mystical practice demands incessant repetition because it contradicts direct experience. Therefore, the phenomenal world is steadfastly dismissed as negligible, and the anchorite endeavors to ignore it, imagining that it does not exist. Through scrupulous introversion the mystic experiences the human essence as the ultimate authenticity. But self-absorption and esoteric reverie do not provide an impartial perspective towards reality because they are experiential practices that are only, inwardly directed. However, cognition through the aegis of the human, intrinsic singularity recognizes all things for their distinctiveness, and consequently, it is considerably more meaningful. Thereby, self-indulgent complacency is avoided because the human essence is established as the perspective from which one engages phenomena and not an experiential end unto itself.

Immediate cognition by the human, essential identity involves and culminates in the direct experience of how things are in reality. When reality is directly experienced through the human quintessence, it becomes clear that formerly, we were restricted to merely an undistinguished evaluation of phenomena. The abstract rationalization of physical evidence was deemed the apogee of cognition because we were ignorant of our innate capacity of direct, cognitive engagement. But the immediate approach provides us with definitive knowledge regarding the intrinsic nature of phenomena and their intangible significances while abstract conceptualization of itself does not engage actual existence. It discusses it remotely endeavoring to come to terms with phenomena through the evaluation of remotely derived information. In this regard, direct experience through the human, intrinsic identity is of an entirely different caliber because it involves the immediate experience of a phenomenon, as it exists, in its entirety.

The human, essential singularity has the capacity, through immediate, experiential cognition to recognize the essence of other phenomena because essential identities are incorporeally significant, and of a like tenor to the human essence. The human, essential identity can discern that which is of like nature. Hence, the human, singular identity discerns the intrinsic significance of all other things.

The intrinsic significance or essential identity of something, while readily discovered through immediate engagement, is more easily discerned through comparison. But is it not by the comparison of the physical properties of something that the essential distinction between two similar phenomena is determined. For example, if the native-element-minerals, gold and copper are compared physically it may be found that they differ only in a piece-meal fashion, but the essential distinction remains elusive. In order to discover the identity of copper, it must be engaged as it exists elementally. This is achieved when the human, essential identity is established as the perspective from which the object is directly engaged.

In fact, the human, essential identity already exists in a condition populated with qualitative distinctions that it can potentially, readily discern. Thus, the intrinsic identity of gold or copper is qualitatively particular, and it is the particular nature of the existence of the one metal that is compared to that of another in order to ascertain the essential manner of expression.

The significance of experiential cognition in order to acquire knowledge, lies in its direct approach. Through immediate encounter, qualities are recognized that remain elusive by an analysis of the merely physical properties. But the direct approach must be established from the perspective of the human, essential identity otherwise direct experience is merely heightened observation. But heightened observation cannot discover the qualitative distinction of something because that capacity is inherent to the incorporeal condition of the human ipseity, which exists only in a condition where essences, but not appearances, are significant. Phenomenal intrinsicality is discovered through the perspective of the human, essential singularity because both are similarly elemental, existing in the same condition of immediacy.

Conventionally, we compare and associate new information with preconceptions and recollections of similarities and then we engage our reason to test them upon that basis. This practice is radically superseded by the discipline of direct engagement, whereby phenomena, through the aegis of the human quintessence, are encountered immediately and essentially.

Knowledge achieved through dialectics is never definitive because the dynamic of matching, comparing and evaluating relies upon deduction as the final arbiter, whose function is necessarily indirect. Furthermore, practices such as the reduction and analysis of physical properties into finer details, offer little improvement because they fail to reveal the qualitatively distinct, intrinsic identity of the entirety.

The intrinsic distinction of an object cannot be discovered definitively by conventional means because profound existence is not found in the physical semblance of itself but only by implication. Therefore, the qualitative distinction of something is incompatible with intellectual evaluation concerning it. The first is discovered immediately while indirect appraisal is concerned with information regarding something but remains ignorant of the essential identity. That is to say, the intellect is incapable of discovering essential existence because of its indirect manner of functioning.

The cognitive capacity whereby an entirety is recognized for its essential significance, and consequently, definitively distinguished, is not cerebral rationalism but immediate encounter. The human, incorporeal essence engages the phenomena directly. It is here that the intellect hesitates because the influence of abstract deduction becomes, of necessity, significantly decreased. Definitive knowledge through direct cognition is inconceivable to the intellect. Additionally, the validity of experiential cognition cannot be successfully argued because it is substantiated and corroborated only through experiential usage. The intellect stumbles when the authenticity of something cannot be demonstrated through reasoning.

Experiential cognition through the application of the human, incorporeal identity is self-validating because it is the direct experience by one absolute reality with another. The human quintessence recognizes its own authenticity through a direct engagement with itself. This essential identification is the foundation of definitive knowledge. Thereby, the human quintessence is indisputably recognized to be real because it is directly

176

self-experienced in a condition that is discovered to be real through the immediacy of our engagement. It is the intellect that is remote, and abstract rationalism that is delayed, and it is analysis and reduction that are distant and isolated practices removed from an immediate experience of the phenomenon. But there is no cognitive separation between the human quintessence and its own particular condition. Thus, immediately ascertained circumstances are not evaluated or reasoned but one they are known directly and experientially. Furthermore, when the attention of the human, essential identity is directed towards other phenomena it recognizes a similarly authentic distinction that is the quintessential identity of the object. That is to say, the human quintessence engages phenomena immediately and discovers intrinsic identities that are not physically identifiable.

The authenticity of the essential identity, as the incorporeal existence of the human being, may only be, at the most, implied through reason. But if rationalism is replaced with cognition through experiential engagement, the existence of the human, essential identity is immediately justified. In other words, abstract rationalism is the wrong faculty for identifying intangible existence. Indeed, the disdain of the materialist for incorporeal significances may be overcome through persuasive argument, but unless the cognitive approach is immediate, and the perspective originates from the

177

human essential identity, nothing is definitively known. That is to say, there is nothing physical that can qualify intangible realities and, consequently, the justification of a position may only be argued abstractly. Therefore, the human quintessence is the vital prerequisite to immediate cognition because without intermediary interpretation, the view of the ipseity is entirely objective. Otherwise, we merely continue in the same state that the abstract rationalist persistently espouses.

The materialist will prefer to attribute the human, essential identity to the physical brain, ascribing in most imaginative ways all significance to that organ. Thereby, the abstract rationalist, incapable of achieving definitive knowledge because it is only achievable through immediate experience, denies the human being the capacity of direct cognition. Unable to justify something that is without physical existence or to qualify a condition through abstract rationalism, the materialist completely denies its significance and conveniently attributes origin to the effect.

Incorporeal, essential identities are qualitatively incommensurate with the faculties of reason. To illustrate this point one has only to consider the materialistic distinction between the conditions of sunrise and sunset. The rationalist attributes an excess of blue light to sunrise, while sunset is differentiated by red light waves. The qualitative distinction is overlooked entirely. The rising of the sun in the morning sky is qualitatively distinct from the descent towards nightfall. Similarly, a singer or musician practicing the scales recognizes a distinction between the ascending notes and the descendant, even though the notes themselves are identical. When the notes are entirely rearranged, a beautiful melody ensures. The differences between the identical sounds and their sequence and tempo alter the qualitative result.

The event of sunrise is qualitatively distinct from the occasion of sunset. The materialist attempts to attribute the distinction to an elusive physical property but merely establishes a remote abstraction. But through immediate engagement, the human, essential identity recognizes the unique quality of sunrise and distinguishes its qualitative significance. The skilled artist articulates the precise nature of the qualitative conditions of the phenomena and successfully reveals their authenticity through voice, movement or color.

Through movement the dancer does not represent sunrise by falling to the ground but rises heavenward with the vitality of a new dawn. Sunset, however, possesses the quality of steadily ebbing activity and of relaxation and tranquility.

Abstract rationalism disdains experientially recognized qualities that are otherwise intangible. Reason cannot attribute significance to them except begrudgingly when they are so blatantly obvious that they cannot be otherwise denied. Indeed, the most disciplined and systematic dialectic can scarcely justify qualitatively distinct, intrinsic identities. The existence of an intangible dimension to reality would have to rest merely upon belief if the cognitional resource for its justification lay only with the reasoning faculties. That is, the existence of incorporeal significances cannot be reasonably demonstrated, but they are known conclusively through immediate, experiential engagement.

The consideration of phenomena upon the basis of physical appearances and their properties and the elaboration of information through deduction will always remain remote from actual and direct experience. Preoccupied with figuring things out and establishing conceptual interpretations, our thinking becomes abstractly preoccupied. Needless to say, concepts that evaluate and define phenomena cannot replace immediate, practical knowledge. But materialism selects the construct over immediate experience because the significance of direct engagement by the authentic, human identity is not regarded as a satisfactorily vindicated option. It is imagined that the justification for the notion of incorporeal significance rests merely upon belief or faith in a mystical revelation. Rationalizing phenomenal appearances, we become convinced that our conceptualizations take ultimate precedence over any other perspective. This is exacerbated as we become steadily convinced that our indirect, abstract evaluation of the world is the optimum, cognitive approach. Consequently, without serious inquiry, we summarily dismiss anything that remotely pertains to intangible dimensionality.

The writings of René Descartes (1596—1650) were significant in an era when humanity was held in an insidious stranglehold of overzealous ecclesiastical dogma, compounded by a legacy of ubiquitous superstition. But his meditations have established, and perpetuated into our own time, a materialistic obliqueness, contrary to Descartes' original purpose. Through profound introspection Descartes discovered and introduced the concept of experientially achieved knowledge of the human, intrinsic identity, but nevertheless, maintained a personal devotion to Deity.

Mostly these two positions have become neglected by modern, materialistic atheism. However, his exposition of the reasoning nature of the human mind as the optimum, cognitive practice able to decipher the physical appearances of existence, remained enthusiastically supported. Descartes did not recognize the dynamic whereby the individual, through direct cognition, essentially cognizant of the existence of an inherent authenticity, similarly possesses the capacity to recognize the intrinsic identity of all external phenomena. Had he realized this capacity he would not have embarked upon an exploration of reason as the sole arbiter of definitive knowledge. It would have been clearly inadequate and unnecessary because he would have already recognized the value of immediate cognition and of his own essential existence.

Descartes experientially recognized his own intrinsic and inviolable distinction. Regarding the phenomenal world he was at a loss because by comparison, nature appeared markedly deficient and qualitatively alien. Thus, he challenged its significance and abstractly questioned the validity of sensory experience, establishing contradictory systems of cognition and abstract dialectic in juxtaposition to immediate experience.

Today we are assisted through this impasse by a more comprehensive application of direct cognition in order that all phenomena may be examined for their essential significance. Through an appraisal of particular instances, whereby incorporeal, qualitative significance is experientially justified and known to be authentic, convincing justification is established for further inquiry. This builds a case for direct cognition, and initial results provide a glimpse of a profoundly more significant dimension to life than merely the physical and superficial appearances.

Descartes' experience reveals that recognition of the human, essential distinction alone, is inadequate because it is not a relevant end in itself. However, applied as an experiential perspective, it offers a foundation of cognitive autonomy. The human essence becomes the authority of the human constitution, from whose perspective authentic identities are straightforwardly recognized.

The plight of the mystic, as stated earlier, is self-absorption, and it is of little value to us because it is a static experience. Isolated and indulged as a euphoric extravagance, experiential knowledge of the existence of the human unique selfhood cannot enhance human autonomy unless it is established as the seat of cognition. That is, cognitive liberation is readily achievable through the human quintessence, but not through self-indulgence. Therefore, the authority of the human, essential distinction must be established as the perspective from which all things are profoundly recognized. Thereby, the human quintessence can recognize the ipseity of others and, similarly, engage the world through immediate cognition to discover the essential significance of all phenomena.

14. THE ESSENTIAL CONDITION OF EXISTENCE

The qualitative expression of the existence of things underlies the facade that is the most familiar and characteristic phenomenal circumstance. Conversely, the obvious semblance is only the most inconsequential aspect if it is considered separately from the intrinsic significance that is represented by the entirety. Nevertheless, if we were to scrutinize the material periphery and analyze the structure of its construction, it would seem as if we had discovered the greater merit of the manifestation. In fact, through detailed physical examination we do not delve deeper in terms of understanding the substantive nature, but merely discover more concerning the carapace.

Habituated as we are with the material perspective, inevitably our view towards existence is shallow, and to the degree that we overemphasize the obvious structure, our understanding is correspondingly is inconsequential. Accordingly, life is more or less meaningless depending on the profundity of our approach.

An insightful understanding of the substantive proportion of the existence of things is vital to a meaningful appreciation of life because otherwise we merely engage the periphery that is of little consequence. Indeed, the shallow, exterior view lacks both the significance and relevance that the essential human being finds worthwhile. Consequently, a superficial existence is inevitably empty of consequence and purpose.

In fact, if we exclusively dwell upon the material conditions of things we only ever discover more of the same both in terms of a hollow existential understanding and the paucity of a worthwhile inner life.

In the circumstances, one would imagine that the highest human priority would concern the discovery of the consequential nature of phenomena and the pursuit of essential knowledge. But, unfortunately, humanity is at an impasse because we do not realize either the existence of a more profound dimension to phenomenal existence, or if we do, we do not know how to survey it.

The substantive proportion of things correspond with the similarly essential nature of the human being. In other words, if we discern the fundamental significance of things, we do so through our own similarly quintessential distinction. Therefore, somehow we must deepen the human perspective from a cursory view and superficial understanding in order to engage the worthwhile volume wherein consequence resides.

The human essential distinction can become established as the primary perspective towards all other things including our fellow human beings. Towards that end, it is possible to consolidate our attention through exhaustive introspection and begin to directly engage circumstances from the view of individual selfhood. However, the tendency towards egocentrism is a very real enticement that works regressively against the development of the human being. In other words, if a powerful moral ethos has not become principally settled within the human heart, the aforementioned approach will benefit us nothing.

Nevertheless, the certain knowledge of intrinsic existence encourages meaningful progress through the awareness of a more profound existence. Consequently, the straightforward approach whereby we restrain an overactive mind and feeling-sentient nature serves us, equally as well. Thereby, when thinking, feeling evaluation and preconception are postponed the human essential ipseity naturally becomes the outstanding perspective.

This seems a very straightforward approach, and indeed, providing we are certain of our objective we can discover the greater profundity of things. Thereby, we find that a solely materialistic interpretation of life is an abstract and superficial human construct. Be that as it may, the intellect endeavors the formulation of existence in functional and utilitarian terms because it is in its nature to do so, and furthermore, the material offers concrete evidence of existence. Nevertheless, reason functions indirectly and does not sufficiently identify intangible factors because they require direct experience in order to be explicitly understood. This establishes a contradiction between the mental picture and knowledge derived through immediate experience.

However, we typically select the conceptual device

over experiential knowledge because it seems to explain existence decisively. Unfortunately, it does so only in the most superficial term, and much that seems reasonable from an intellectual point of view remains erroneous. Thus, the consequence of an excessive reliance upon rationale is an artificial evaluation of life that does not resemble experiential reality.

Nevertheless, as qualities are undeniably recognized as extant through direct observation, their significance may be tacitly reintroduced as a factor, even of an exclusively materialistic philosophy. But the human essence alone has the capacity to recognize qualitative significance because it engages phenomena immediately. Also, immediacy is the immanent condition wherein the intrinsic significance of things becomes known. But the intellect cannot obliquely fathom what qualities actually signify because of their intangible nature. Accordingly, only the immediate engagement of phenomena by the human essence reveals the intrinsic identities that make up a profound and meaningful existence.

In other words, the colors red, blue and yellow are qualitatively distinct from one another. The human essence recognizes the intrinsic identity of each through immediate engagement. Thereby, each color is identified essentially for its unique singularity, and it is the qualitative distinction between them that identifies the substantive particularity of the color.

The discovery of the essential identity of a

phenomenon through immediate engagement by the human essence and the recognition of the singular distinction of a thing as its authentic condition of existence, shows the inadequacy of an only materialistic explication of life. Yet, the materialist remains unconvinced through dialectic. Nevertheless, it is crucial that these things be explored experientially because they cannot be otherwise appreciated; and consequently our perspective remains too shallow.

The first step is the restraint of intellectual and sentimental evaluation in order that the human, essential identity may be positioned as the sole, cognitive authority. Subsequently, the qualitative distinction of the phenomenon is immediately engaged by the essential individual. Thereby, the human, incorporeal identity, recognizes the equally intangible, essential significance of a phenomenon as the most profound condition of an objects' existence.

As previously stated, in terms of the capacity to clearly distinguish identities through experiential observation is assisted when phenomena are qualitatively compared one with another. Subsequently, it is immediately apparent through comparison that, while objects have obvious physical differences, the distinction between them is more profoundly determined through an examination of their qualitative expression.

If we examine examples of native-element-minerals that occur in nature in uncombined form, comparing them in the same manner as we engaged variations in the qualitative identity of colors, again we recognize that their distinctions are profoundly qualitative and not merely physical. But we cannot adequately capture dispositional quality through chemical analysis, a numerical position on the scale of hardness or by scrutiny of the physical structure. Furthermore, in order to communicate the intrinsic nature of something we have to resort to the vernacular of the artist. Indeed, this is typically the case of all intangible significances.

The qualitative nature of something cannot be adequately identified merely through physical metrics. The native-element-mineral, copper, is described by the metallurgist in terms of its physical properties. However, copper possesses a qualitative distinction that is its authentic identity. Experientially, a particular significance is engaged that must be portrayed figuratively to be communicated. A literal description, established rigidly upon the material condition or through an analysis of the physical aspects alone, cannot reveal the qualitative singularity because material evidence and incorporeal significance are of incommensurate existence except in terms of the superficial view and the profound.

When we strive to know the nature or identity of a phenomenon from a qualitative point of view, we must set aside intellectual and sentimental activity in order that the human essence can engage the situation without preconception. Any prejudice will detract from the

190

immediate experience and compromise our results. The human essence must engage the object directly without interference to apprehend its independent circumstances. Direct cognition should not be confused with endeavoring to feel what an object is or how the object seems to be. That practice is not direct cognition but an activity of heightened, subjective appraisal such as animal instinct and feeling sentience. It may be astute under the best of circumstance, but typically it involves a muddied introspection as equally remote from reality as that of abstract thinking or mysticism. So often, the apparent revelations are falsifiable and severely open to abuse.

The practice of direct, experiential cognition results in definitive knowledge because it immediately involves intrinsic realities. It requires the application of the human, essential singularity which experientially recognizes its own authenticity, and discerns the essential identity of the object of interest. When we turn the gaze of our essence towards an object to discover its inherent particularity, we set aside rationale and sentimental activity. Thereby, in present timing phenomena, are recognized not for the transient and superficial appearances that so dismayed Descartes, but for their intrinsic, qualitative distinctions. Qualitative distinctions are revealed as the profound identity of phenomena.

The artist endeavors to articulate the authentic, intrinsic circumstances of a situation because they cannot be otherwise portrayed through conventional classification, which require a physical presence. Thus, we directly engage different colors or native-element-minerals and discern their qualities endeavoring to articulate their essential condition. But we cannot do this by describing them in terms of their physical appearance because qualitative distinctions are intangible.

A merely subjective evaluation is of no use to us either. Our preferences and feelings cannot objectively identify qualitative distinctions. The human essence must engage the phenomenon immediately to experience the essential distinction. Nothing short of this will reveal the authentic condition of phenomenal existence.

In other words, the qualitative distinctions of phenomena possess an intrinsic significance that is not revealed by the physical circumstances. They exist as the essential singularity and identification of an object. This is a juxtaposed position from materialism. Materialism insists that the physical appearance is the entirety and consequently it marginalizes qualities, dismissing them because they have no tangible significance. But, through immediate engagement by the human, essential identity, qualitative distinctions are recognized for their extant existence and materialism is revealed as a fundamentally flawed and a perversely distorted perspective towards life.

15. RECOGNIZING ESSENTIAL DISTINCTION

We dwell physically within the world, and we are, with it, an expression of the genius of its inception, development and maintenance. But, unlike plants and animals, we also possess the capacity of self-consciousness. Therefore, it is an extraordinary thing to recognize, through immediate experience, the existence of one's own intrinsic uniqueness.

Thereupon, we directly engage the phenomenon of our own identity and experientially discern that we ourselves are actually real, as a singular distinction. In this connection, we qualify the existence of our authentic person through an immediate event of self-recognition. Further, we recognize that others possess a similar uniqueness. Indeed, in the same manner whereby we discovered that qualitative distinctions are the authentic identity of natural phenomena; we recognize that our own mutual essential identity exists elementally.

Human nature is fashioned in order to be potentially capable of great creative works, and we can also compose compound and complex conceptualizations. Thus, we are of two natures. The physical we share with other organisms, while the essential identity remains incorporeal and akin to the genius that perpetuates the working intricacies of organic viability. In other words, we possess both physicality and incorporeal existence.

The intrinsic human being is incorporeal and correspondingly identifiable through our activities of conceptualization and volition. Thus, through extension, we discern the existence of an elemental condition wherein entities are determined not by their physical appearances, but through the intrinsic uniqueness of their identity and by their labors.

Yet, less we become immodest, it should be remembered that we did not fashion ourselves and while our creativity is inherent to our constitution, everything the human being makes from the things of the Earth already exists in potential. The laws that we discover and then reapply to our advantage are not of our establishment. Thus, we seem independent but in reality we work within definite parameters.

But through self-recognition, we discover that we possess the potential of intrinsic and cognitive liberty. Our latent autonomy resides within the extraordinary, intrinsic uniqueness of our identity. That is to say, our essential singularity, that is recognized as authentic through immediate cognition, enjoys a condition of independence founded upon the incorporeal existence of our individual uniqueness.

We further recognize that, although at present we are in a condition of cognitive limitation, yet through our incorporeal nature we are endowed with the potential of independence through direct knowledge of things as they essentially exist and upon the establishment of an appropriate moral ethos.

For the same reason, cognitive autonomy preemptively resides within our innate capacity to recognize the authenticity of our own intrinsic identity and the essential existence of other phenomena. For this reason, recognition of definitive distinction, which is the absolute identity of things, provides us with discretional liberty to engage phenomena judiciously because we know things as they actually are.

This means, through the direct engagement of the human essence, we encounter the reality of things because we apprehend then immediately. Immediate, cognitive occupation with a circumstance, from the perspective of the permanence of the human singularity, necessarily reveals its authentic condition through the direct manner of our engagement.

Therefore, we do not have to remain content with half knowledge nor rely upon the educated speculations of our reasoning faculties. Neither are we limited to belief and faith, but we can know things immediately for what they are through our innate capacity of artless and straightforward engagement.

When a situation is immediately engaged we encounter the volume of existence wherein the authentic nature of things becomes evident. Thereby, the human, essential singularity discerns the intrinsic identity of everything within its focus. But, in order to discover the authenticity of something we approach the experience questioningly from the perspective of the human essence and not intellectually through our cerebral faculty. We engage directly and silently with something as if we had no prior knowledge. We engage it originally, and in this manner, we discover the authentic distinction and inherent significance or profound nature of the phenomenon.

The human, innate capacity to determine things as they originally exist allows us to discover the incorporeal significances of things. This reveals an entirely different dimension to existence than that achieved through a scrutiny of merely physical properties. However, immediate engagement must be established as an authentic experience in order to be of value. While an alternative cognitive approach may be conceptually enticing, reasonably argued and persuasive, entertaining merely another abstraction is completely pointless.

The entire significance of the immediate engagement of phenomena through the aegis of the human, essential identity is that we thereby enter a condition wherein everything is discovered for its authenticity. This approach is not a system or a methodology but a cognitive approach whereby the extant condition of something is directly encountered.

We have already discussed how the world is significantly misrepresented when physical aspects are isolated from the qualitative significances of phenomena and considered separately, and exclusively. The isolation and analysis of solely the material aspects misinterprets the world as if it were composed exclusively of those palpable parts. We recognized how mechanistic, a cold and inhumane a depiction founded exclusively upon tangibility is and how remote it is from experiential knowledge of the qualitative dimension of existence. It is a fabrication that we have established for ourselves but it is not essentially real. The missing constituent is the intangible significances of phenomena.

But while we may conceptually reintroduce qualities into our world-view, it is the immediate experience of them that is significant. The incorporeal dimension of existence wherein qualitative significances reside is not something eccentric but it is familiar to everyone experientially. But materialistic theory contradicts that experiential knowledge. Consequently, the addition of the qualitative significances of phenomena as viable and meaningful evidence concerning existence may yet remain merely an intellectual exercise.

That which is lacking from the exclusively physical, contrived world-view maintained by materialistic Western philosophy, is dimensionality. The missing dimension is the profound and the manner whereby it is recognized for its authenticity, is immediate engagement. Thus, the qualitative distinction of something signifies what it inherently is while the physical properties are the attributes that belong to the carapace. That is to say, identity is intrinsic, and intrinsicality is known through direct experience, while knowledge concerning it arises through the perspective of the human, essential identity.

Abstract, philosophical rationalism demonstrates the extraordinary capacity of the human, cerebral faculty to conjure interminable permutations of information, manipulating multiple expositions and assessing them through oblique dialectic. But a philosophical position established upon reasoned exposition can never be definitively justified, despite impressive erudition, because in the final analysis, it will always remain indirectly conceived. That is to say, a conclusive argument can never reveal profundity because while the intellect exhaustively deduces through sequential, logical argument the merits of a position, it cannot directly engage a phenomenon. Intrinsic meaningfulness is only discerned through immediate engagement, but the intellect is necessarily indirect in its approach. Inevitably preoccupied with indirect information respecting phenomena, it is incapable of direct engagement.

The incapacity of the intellect to definitively recognize essential, phenomenal identity is founded upon its manner of functioning. Reason is an organ that evaluates but essential, phenomenal identity is intrinsic and incorporeal, and cannot be calculated without specific computable data. Consequently, immediate apprehension is required by the intrinsic and incorporeal identity of the human being in order that the crucial volume of things be recognized.

The confusion, whereby human identity is relegated to a physical organ that only functions indirectly, and the human essential singularity is, similarly, denied existence, is devastating in the imprisoning effect it has upon human consciousness. Convinced that our highest faculty of cognition is the indirectly functioning brain, we apply similar metrics towards the rest of existence.

But reason is a specialized and limited faculty that is unable to identify a state or condition of existence that is without physical parameters. That is to say, rationale does not experience, but essential conditions can only be discovered experientially.

However, if we explore the direct approach, recognizing the restricted nature of reason predisposed as it is to computation, we avoid abstract supposition. We discover that immediate engagement reveals qualitative significances that are beyond the capacity of deduction to evaluate. Indeed, it is the intangible, qualitative distinctions of phenomena that are the authentic identity, and the elemental condition of phenomena are recognized when the human being engages existence immediately and discovers their definitive condition.

A direct engagement between the human, essential identity and natural phenomena reveals the qualitative distinction of an organism as its quintessential identity. In fact, the intrinsic nature of an organism remains true to its identity even if some of its physical attributes are eliminated. If we remove some of the legs of a spider it, yet remains a spider. What we have done through our exclusively materialistic mentality, is to assume that the identity of the spider consists of its attributes: its legs or its appearance. If little by little every trace of the spider but one detail were removed, nonetheless, its identity would remain consistent.

The essential distinction is the authentic identity, but not the physical appearance. That is to say, if we merely view the carapace, we overlook the authentic nature that continues even if one half of the insect were removed to a different location. Indeed, the same identity could be different situated in several places. This is because intrinsic distinctions, being incorporeal are not contingent for their existence upon space. The actual identity is more significant than the physical properties, and it is this essential existence that we confront through the direct engagement of a phenomenon by the similarly incorporeal, human existence.

The theory that the concept of an object is more significant than its appearance has been around since Plato. The difference here is that we are not conceptualizing. There is no advantage in further embellishing a concept that has long since lost its original significance. The condition we are presenting involves an experiential manner of cognition that enables the human being to recognize the full existence of phenomena including the human, essential identity. It is not an abstract idea but an existential condition.

In the same vein, the significance of intangibles such as essential identity, archetypal organization or qualitative distinctions may be further illustrated by returning briefly to the subject of organic metamorphosis. An organic form will metamorphose through alternate appearances, yet, its identity always remains the same. That is because the changing appearance of an organism does not alter the intrinsic distinction. The qualitative significance that determines the intrinsic identity of a butterfly remains consistent whether represented as egg, chrysalis or flying insect. Thus, the appearance will alter according to the necessity of the archetypal principle of metamorphosis, yet the intrinsic identity remains consistent.

The particular identity is of greater significance than the appearance. For example, two different varieties of butterfly observed side by side are differentiated through the qualitative distinction of their interpretation of a common, lepidopteran concept. Therefore, the significance of the insect lies less in the appearance and more pertinently in the qualitatively distinct manner in which the butterfly conceptualization is realized.

Similarly, the vastly complex, compound organization of the organic archetype is composed towards specific ends through the aegis of intention and volition. This purposefulness is easily recognized through the observation of the myriad intricacies enacted towards a certain, immaculate accomplishment.

The difference between the consequence of a capricious act and determined activity directed towards a specific end lies in the practicality of its operations towards a compound result. If there was merely a chaotic result to an action one could easily claim that there was no intention. But, random actions are typically destructive rather than creative. Spontaneous organization would require the impossible collusion of myriad, unproductive forces. But when we recognized an established progression whereby, a creature transforms through numerous appearances towards a specific culmination then purpose is clearly indicated.

In other words, the complex arrangement of sequentially related activities achieves a very specific and practical result. That is, when an activity is recognized to be the fulfillment a complex and successful synthesis of achievements such as egg, chrysalis and butterfly, including the dynamic of reproduction, then systematically established structures, established through intention and volition, are most assuredly in evidence. In that case, in terms of organic life, intricate activities are performed in order to achieve the specific end of a viable, life cycle of growth, development and reproduction. Further, ecological influences are taken into consideration. Through provocation, they introduce variations to the qualitative distinction which is the qualitative expression of the existence of the organism. The identity of the creature changes and is consequently refashioned in appearance becoming increasingly appropriate in nature with respect to ecological demands. Thus, qualitatively, the creature becomes progressively alike to a specific ecological context. That is a creature belongs to a habitat, and visa versa. Thereupon, the existing manner of organic interpretation and the qualitative distinction of future generations is altered accordingly.

When it is recognized that the qualitative distinction of an organism is the authentic identity, then, it becomes self-evident that the incorporeal particularity precedes the manner of appearance. The determined materialist will maintain that the physical appearance attributes identity and not the intrinsic quality that differentiates one phenomenon from another. In this regard, in terms of archetypal organization as the conceptualization of complex, metamorphosing arrangements, the materialist will admit to no distinction between capricious cause and effect on the one hand, and the measured approach towards a definitive objective.

This is because the materialistic perspective is exclusive. It only cedes validity to physical conditions and natural forces. Thus, through determined imagination it is supposed that random causes produce organization of vast, metamorphic complexity. Indeed, remote, abstract thinking extracts information piece-meal from circumstances, mulls and balances details remotely from the occurrence in order to build a case for spontaneity.

Thus, the materialistic evolutionary perspective is skewed obliquely in every regard. The consequences of random action by capricious forces is always chaos. We know this from our own experience. Furthermore, compound, practical results do not issue from mayhem. Consequently, we recognize the position of the determined materialist as speculative and abstractly contrived. Occupied exclusively with data derived from physical appearances and established upon abstract rationalism, it is a fabricated conceptualization, remote from reality. Further, the recognition of the dynamic of metamorphosis itself entirely discredits the postulate of complexity arising from random action. This, is because intentional motivation is implied by the very existence of metamorphosis. In other words, metamorphosis is a deliberate dynamic of considerable complexity that cannot be considered capricious because the random convergence of matter with physical forces possesses no such sophistication.

However, the observer who immediately engages the phenomenon itself, experiences it as it exists in reality and is not misled by abstract speculation. Through the recognition of intention towards the realization of the dynamic of organic life, a glimpse is possible of the activity of archetypal composition. Conceptualization, volition and realization are readily recognizable indicators of significant purposefulness. Indeed, without conceptualization there is no organization. Nevertheless, organization is everywhere in evidence and particularly demonstrated through metamorphosis.

Conception and volition are familiar incorporeal, human activities and no one seriously denies their reality or significance. Yet, organisms of astonishing complexity, progress through one metamorphic reestablishment after another towards the realization of a specific end, nevertheless, the materialist attributes the dynamic of transformation to mere caprice.

The archetype of metamorphic reformation exists as an undifferentiated compound of interrelationships and re-expressions whereby a cycle of transformations is physically realized through the vivifying qualities of the supportive and nourishing agencies of life. Therefore, dynamic organization is the imperative of every organic expression. But, there is little purpose in presenting further evidence because of the vulnerability of the intellect to abstraction. In order to explore and verify the existence of intangible realities it is necessary to directly experience them oneself. The intellect works in an entirely different manner from experiential cognition and must be restrained in order that the human, essential identity may encounter phenomena directly, without the interference of dialectic and abstract evaluation.

16. INTRINSIC SIGNIFICANCE

The qualities of phenomena are experientially evident, but their intangible nature renders them almost indescribable in conventional terms. It is challenging to represent the qualitative distinction between two colors or to describe the quality of a rosy apple, freshly picked from the tree. We imagine that an object is usually identified through physical associations that are recalled through the application of a name. But interestingly, we are just as likely to associate something with a qualitative memory. We recognize that qualities such as the freshness of air, the early morning avian chorus or moonlight are known experientially and require an expressive description in order to be communicated and that they are not successfully represented through physical association. However, careful observation of our associations reveals that a significant proportion of our mental connections involve not exclusively physical properties, as the materialist would have us believe, but medleys of predominantly qualitative significances.

Scientific discipline requires exactitude of communication and a systematic, inflexible approach that is analytical in nature. Phenomena are painstakingly described in terms of their physical properties and evaluated exclusively upon the basis of their material existence. In the quest to discover their intrinsic identity, phenomena are scrutinized piecemeal, the functioning investigated to the finest detail and their physical condition meticulously reduced to minutiae.

Materialistic, Western philosophy endeavors to imitate the rigid discipline of science and, similarly emphasize material appearances in an attempt to evaluate existence upon solid, physical evidence. This is then taken to excess through further, abstract conjecture so that the resulting depiction of life only remotely resembles our direct experience.

The difficulty is that existence is not composed solely of physical properties but possesses a significant qualitative dimension. The qualitative dimension is unmanageable through the scientific approach and, consequently, theories and hypotheses concerning existence are floated that are devoid of qualitative content.

The paradox between physical appearances and essential significance is scarcely recognized, while the denial of merit to qualitative existence has become a steadily more entrenched mentality. The contradiction between the materialistic depiction of the world fortified by the scientific approach and experiential engagement has become an acceptable conundrum. Increasingly, the pertinence of the qualitative dimension of existence is diminished and disregarded as something not seriously real but subjective and imaginative.

However, it is the qualitative nature that reveals the intrinsic distinction and significance between phenomena. While the properties of the physical appearance present merely superficial and peripheral evidence.

A color represented as the numerical value of a certain wavelength of light, or a cool morning breeze from the ocean described in terms of its temperature, water content and chemical composition, offers very inadequate, essential information. Unfortunately, materialistic, Western philosophy maintains, according to extraordinarily banal reasoning, that the quantifiable properties of an object exist as the concrete reality. Of itself, this position is easily identified as the inevitable consequence of an abstract rationalism that declares only the physical appearance of a phenomenon to be authentic. This is because physical appearances possess tangible and readily assimilable data, while the existence of qualitative significances must be experientially authenticated. Thus, we have taken the easily accommodated information as exclusively valid.

Consequently, materialism has become firmly established within the Western philosophic and scientific community and forced upon our culture through the assumed authority of an intellectual elite. Materialism is considered the exclusively, viable approach towards phenomenal existence and forms the basis of our understanding of existence. However, when phenomena are directly and experientially engaged, this perspective is found to be far removed from reality.

We explore the distinctions between phenomena for their qualitative singularity and know their intrinsic identities through direct cognition even though we may not have the necessary skill to articulate their individuation. Nevertheless, one engages them first-hand and it is folly to negate their significance. To do so reduces existence to a mere shadow of reality.

Unacknowledged by the materialist is the importance of the qualitative dimension of existence, not merely in the usual adjectival sense as a qualifier of the material condition, but as the significant distinction between phenomena. The color yellow, for example, is recognized to possess an extant distinction that exists separately from a physical context. That is, the individual color has an intrinsic identity of its own that is independent of its material circumstances.

As we experientially explore the impressiveness of the qualitative characteristics and identities of phenomena, we become aware that life is elementally composed of qualitatively differentiated existences. Further, we find through immediate engagement that essential distinctions exists as the intrinsic condition of phenomena. Yet, we have become preoccupied with a superficial and abstract perspective towards life, never fully engaged or cognizant of how things are in reality. But the impoverished, materialistic perspective is superseded through the immediate recognition of a dimension of existence that is entirely more significant.

The qualitative distinction between phenomena such as the color yellow or red, engaged as separate entities independently of their physical establishment, are found to be distinguishable through their inherent identities. They possess a singular significance that remains consistent regardless of where or how they are found. That is, yellow or red are always distinguished for their particular qualitative significance, but the qualitative uniqueness that distinguishes essential identities cannot be described in physical terms because they are without physical properties. Consequently, they are identified through immediate engagement from the perspective of the human, essential identity, while their existence can be metaphorically and figuratively described and authenticated through articulate, artistic mastery.

Direct cognition through the aegis of the human essence, enables the observer to engage the unique, individual nature of an object immediately, for what it is, as a straightforward experience. The legitimate identity of the human being, although intangible engages its own authentic identity experientially and recognizes the singularity of the distinction. Further, it determines the essential existence of other human beings and qualitative differentiation as the distinction that distinguishes between phenomena.

We have become accustomed to individualizing phenomena based upon their appearances. However, qualitative intrinsicality and physical appearance are incommensurable perspectives. The authentic identity of a phenomenon is intrinsic, essential and intangible, while the appearance remains variable, comparatively superficial, and without dimensional significance.

Of course, we never experience life without qualities because they are apparent to every physical phenomenon. But materialistic, Western philosophy disregards them and presents a false interpretation of existence as if life were void of qualities. This position is steadfastly maintained through abstract, reasoned exposition and deduced from the exclusive examination of material appearances without their qualitative significances. Thus, a world-view has become established that, while remote from reality is, nonetheless, increasingly adopted as authentic. This fundamental error of perception is enormously detrimental in terms of the way in which we evaluate life and vastly influential upon our perspective towards every aspect of human experience.

Thus, we fail miserably when we attempt to classify phenomena from their mere physical appearances because isolated semblances, devoid of their qualitative dimension, are only partially represented. But intrinsic identity is discovered through direct cognition to be the particular, qualitative distinction of a thing. That is, authentic identity is recognized as the essential singularity of existence and not the merely peripheral condition. Indeed, it is the manner whereby a phenomenon is intrinsically distinguished that determines what it is.

The materialistic perspective as a philosophy replaces qualitative distinctions of existence with physical appearances reducing the richness and profundity of reality to a shallow semblance. But all physical appearances possess qualitative dimensionality which is the authentic distinction between them. If phenomena are consistently evaluated in a merely superficial manner, their authentic condition remains obscure. Consequently, our perception of existence is reduced to one of shallowness and aridity. We no longer know what a thing actually is because we are preoccupied with our conception of it founded upon information concerning the physical appearance.

The practice of immediate cognition whereby phenomena become recognized for their authentic existence, is also the manner whereby we distinguish reality from invention. The former perspective that classified objects according to their physical appearances and properties is revealed as an extraordinarily obscure and shallow interpretation. Rather, we engage life immediately and know all things by the distinction of their original, intrinsic significance. In the place of abstract and indirectly derived information, deduced from the physical properties of phenomena, we know them for their elemental condition. The new approach reveals our former ignorance whereby we evaluated things peripherally and interpreted them based upon intellectual or sentimental preference void of astute recognition. Direct cognition requires neither the interpretation nor the evaluation of phenomena in order to distinguish them but knows them immediately for their intrinsic and singular condition of existence.

We are not content with appearances because we wish to directly know the essential substance of a phenomenon. We wish to know the condition of its existence. Thus, a creature or a plant is not classified according to its material constitution but by virtue of the qualitative distinction of its existential expression.

The identity of a creature is conspicuous through the quality of its nature in much the same way as the color yellow is identified as having extant significance irrespective of context. Thus, the creature physically embodies a particular qualitative expression of the animalian concept. Thereby, the identity of an organism is revealed through its essential demeanor, and the qualitative condition of its existence is recognized as the authentic identity.

Intrinsic identity is more succinctly expressed by the Austrian artist and philosopher, Rudolf Steiner (1861-1925) as the gesture and demeanor (Geste u. Miene) of an animal or plant. That is to say, it is the qualitative condition that distinguishes one organism from another while the appearance is contingent upon its essential significance.

Thus, we recognize the importance of the qualitative nature of phenomena as the significant, yet has overlooked the dimensionality of existence. Water, for example, is identified intrinsically for its qualitative significance through immediate experience but superficially, as consisting of oxygen and hydrogen in a ratio of 2:1. Hydrogen and oxygen are similarly identified by their intrinsic, qualitative distinctions and only superficially determined based upon their physical properties. A grasp of the intrinsic, qualitative identities of each reveals why, in specific combination, their inherent identities combine to establish a substance with the specific quality that epitomizes water. The immediate identification of qualitative significances through direct engagement by the human essence renders the materialistically founded atomic theory, moot. Our perspective is newly established upon the evidence of intrinsic distinctions that comprise the essential, qualitative existence of the phenomenon.

Correspondingly, the dynamic whereby ecological challenges provokes animalian alteration illustrates the significance of qualitative identities. Ecological variance precipitates the adaption of an established organism, but the creature initially alters in terms of its essential distinction. The characteristic demeanor or temperament alters in its stance towards the ecology, and the intrinsic identity adjusts accordingly. This adjustment of nature influences the appearance by stimulating variation that is of the quality of the newly established demeanor. The qualitative distinction of the creature has altered. Therefore, the form adjusts correspondingly because the appearance belies the intrinsic, qualitative identity. Consequently, the creature appears different and, indeed, it is essentially a different animal.

Directly experienced and immediately known qualitative distinctions are determined as authentic to the degree that the human essence confronts phenomena directly and discovers their intrinsic identity. Conventional thinking, that is necessarily remote in comparison, evaluates phenomena indirectly and only superficially. But immediate experience occurs in present timing requiring straightforward engagement. It is the condition of immediacy between the human essence and the phenomenon, that predicates essential reality.

Interestingly, the achievement of direct cognition is recognized as immediate when the phenomenon is three-dimensionally vivid. This is because the object is not abstractly considered from the point of view of cerebral evaluation but immediately engaged. Therefore, the encounter between the human essence and a phenomenon in its three-dimensional condition reveals that the evaluation is no longer remotely or abstractly conducted, but an immediate, unalloyed occurrence in present timing is accomplished. The phenomenon is directly engaged, and its intrinsic significance becomes evident. Accordingly, a unique experience of the circumstances is achieved and, consequently, things become known for their distinctive identity through the similarly authentic uniqueness of the human being.

One is struck by the discrepancy between abstract, evaluative thinking and immediate cognition. The manner whereby the essential dimension of things becomes known does not involve reasoning or calculated appraisal. But, the direct experience of the intrinsic identity of oneself, others and the world offer a liberty of discernment because an unobstructed meeting immediately occurs between the human essence and the object. In this connection, the human essence is able to recognize qualities alike to its own profound significance because it engages their authentic existence.

All things have a constitutional intrinsicality. Experience of the world through direct cognition allows the human being access to a dimension populated with essential distinctions. Physical properties continue although they are recognized as relative and not intrinsic. They are no longer deemed the exclusive evidence of existence. In other words, superficial appearances and abstractly assessed information is insufficient as it fails to include intangible intrinsicality. Indeed, exclusive attention to the material and tangible aspects of phenomena is recognized as an impoverished and unrealistic perspective.

Phenomenal appearances belie the incorporeal dimension of existence which consists of inherent distinctions, qualitative significances and intrinsic identity. The qualitative dimension is composed of essentials that cannot be discovered through a scrutiny of the exclusively physical properties of phenomena or by the application of human rationalism. But the inherent singularity that essentially distinguishes one thing from another is known only through direct cognition. That Is, essential identity is only experientially discernible because of the intangible condition of the existence of the observer and the essential nature of the object of observation.

While we reside in the midsts of qualitative identities, the practice whereby they may be known and justified is, thus far, only vaguely recognized. Direct cognition is muddled together with other unrelated practices and insightful knowledge is thought to be merely capricious. Consequently, we have failed to deliberately and sensibly apply our inherent capacity to immediately engage with the significant identity of things. Instead, we rely upon an indirect evaluation and interpretation founded merely upon the superficial appearances of physical properties or upon no evidence at all. The abstractly conceived inferences that we have adopted as a sufficiently convincing interpretation of existence, remain far from definitive and, furthermore, they are extremely misleading because of their superficial nature.

Distinctions between phenomena are established upon variations in the qualitative significance of their existence. Their qualitative intrinsicality is their authentic identity. In order to apprehend the characteristic particularity of an object the human being must adopt the direct approach. This requires an encounter between the incorporeal identity of the human being, whereby the essential nature of the object is revealed through direct engagement. The human, essential identity acknowledges the authentic condition of the phenomenon and knows it, recognizing that existence is populated not merely with material appearances but with, more significantly, intrinsic realities qualitatively akin to one's own essential identity. It is the incorporeal intrinsicality that is significant because it is the qualitative essence of a thing as opposed to an overestimation of the mere outward appearance.

17. DEFINITIVE COGNITION

The acquisition of definitive knowledge is dependent upon an immediate encounter with phenomena through the essential, human identity. Immediate means in present timing whereby one is directly engaged and immanently cognizant of the phenomenon as opposed to merely abstractly considering it. The intrinsic singularity of the human being engages an object directly and the similarly intrinsic identity of a phenomenon becomes evident.

The human intellect is a faculty and, as such, it is incapable of direct determination and obviously, without quiddity it cannot experience because its function is to reason and evaluate. It is the conviction of the materialist that the cerebral condition of the human constitution is the authentic identity. This is merely an abstractly conceived standpoint. A capacity possesses no essential identity, neither can it directly experience an object because it is an instrument without elemental existence. That is to say, the instrument is not the person.

When the human essence experiences itself through immediate engagement it is correctly identified as the intrinsic identity of the human constitution and the physical is recognized as void of separate significance through the transience of its existence. Furthermore, the authentic identity is able to immediately experience but abstract rationalism remains a function that necessarily performs obliquely.

Reality is a condition that has to be experienced in order to be known, and it cannot be indirectly authenticated through logical elaboration with any meaningful degree of justice. Experientially known essential identities are inaccessible to reason because the intellect is a corporeal faculty of understanding that does not, of itself, possess an individuality that can authenticate anything through direct experience. It can only reason, and reasoning, of necessity, always remains an indirect activity of evaluation. Thus, the possessor of the greater intellect and superior logical facility does not necessarily know reality any better than anyone else.

Similarly, the feeling sentient nature evaluates subjectively. While it may be astute and apparently insightful, the knowledge achieved is not even remotely definitive. Alike to the faculty of reason, affection and presentiment are inappropriately applied in order to discern reality because they offer only instinctive judgment. They can only allude, surmise and indirectly evaluate.

While the intellect is a calculative function, heightened, feeling sentience is a condition alike to the predominant consciousness of the animal kingdom. Neither of these abilities can recognize inherent singularities and identify them because they do not themselves possess that distinction. They are capacities of the human constitution without individuation and consequently, they remain incapable of recognizing the identity of anything else. They possess no essential identity of their own.

Consequently, the intellect and the feelings cannot know the intrinsic identity of a phenomenon because they are qualitatively incommensurate with essential singularities that require immediate engagement in order to be determined. They are functions without requisite identity and cannot therefore recognize the same. Only the human essence is cognitively direct and capable of experientially engaging circumstances. That is to say, the human identity can discern the intrinsic identities of phenomena because it is an entity and not merely a function; it can experience because it possesses the distinction of unique singularity.

The faculty of reason and that of sentimental evaluation are misapplied when directed towards the determination of what constitutes reality because they are inherently incapable of immediate engagement. The intellect can determine the truth or falsehood of a calculation or debate the conformity of a logical position but reality is beyond its capacity to determine because it cannot immediately experience a situation. Thus, reality must be experienced in order to be identified as extant because it is a condition. As such the authenticity cannot be reasoned because it is a qualitative state of existence.

Put differently, reason, as a faculty, requires information that can be sequentially evaluated as true or false. But real and unreal directly authenticate or deny the existence of an event while truth or falsehood only abstractly evaluate an argument.

The consequent distortions of perception through the misapplication of the intellect, in order to attempt a definition of reality, are everywhere evident. The intellect presents an interpretation of the world equivalent to its own functioning and insists that phenomena are entirely composed of properties and attributes that it recognizes and deals with through an inherently, calculative nature. The abstract perspective of the intellect is compounded by further quantitative evidence drawn from the physical appearances of phenomena which only intensify an already remote point of view.

But the intellect cannot directly determine qualitative evidence and cannot abstractly evaluate essential identities because of the oblique and calculative manner of the functioning. Deemed by the materialist, the exclusive, cognitive faculty of the human constitution, it discards experientially derived knowledge because it cannot fathom or justify physically elusive existence without physical metrics. Thus, it does not cede intangibles any significant identity because they cannot be reasoned and calculated nor demonstrated as physically extant. For which reason, recognition of their intrinsic authenticity is beyond its capacity because it functions indirectly and remotely from the event and must have physically derived data to work with.

Similarly, the world-view presented by the human, feeling nature is incapable of evaluating directly apprehended information for its authenticity because it is a subjective faculty of appraisal. It evaluates from the perspective of preference and emotion. But the sentimental perspective is a fickle, temperamental predisposition towards something, swayed impulsively by the demands of corporeality and motivated by impression and sensation. There is no liberty of cognition possible through this approach either.

The human, essential existence identifies phenomena definitively through direct engagement. It is familiar with absolute identities and recognizes essentials alike to itself. The authentic identity of the human being knows the real identity of other entities because the essential distinction of a thing is of the same caliber as the ipseity of the human being. Further, the immediate approach occasions a condition of engagement that exists between the past and the future. It is neither preconceived nor reminiscent and, as such, it is an immanent experience wherein things are discovered in their authentic state of existence. In other words, they are experienced as they exist immediately.

The intellect can determine how a thing works, and may, consequently, reason what it may be, but only based upon those terms. The intellect is a corporeal function and readily recognizes the functioning of other phenomena. Figuring out is the manner of the working.

But the appearance or functioning of an object is not the same as the intrinsic identity. That is to say, the physical properties are not the definition of what something is but how it seems to be from the perspective of the physical appearance. A phenomenon cannot be definitively identified by its semblance because appearances change while the identity of an object remains constant.

The intellect relies upon physical analysis for the identification of an object because it is incapable of recognizing the intrinsic identity which is intangible in nature. Only the authentic identity of the human being can determine intrinsic identities because the human essence exists in a condition of immediacy alike to the state wherein the essential distinction of phenomena resides. This condition of existence is the authentic, spiritual realm.

In order to gather further information to qualify a hypothetical identification founded upon the physical, the intellect must reduce the whole into fractions to facilitate comprehension. Nonetheless, it cannot definitely identify an object regardless of how thoroughly it scrutinizes the material appearance. It merely classifies parts and functions through an analysis of the physical composition. While the myriad aspects and physical details of a phenomenon, revealed through analysis, are imaginatively named, identification, through a scrutiny of the physical appearance, becomes increasingly elusive. Physical analysis inevitably fails to reveal the intrinsic singularity of a phenomenon because the authentic identity of something is the qualitative and elemental distinction that is discovered only through the direct engagement of the human, essential existence.

The deception of a practice wherein the physical details of the entirety are fractionated, labeled and classified, is that the identity of the entirety only appears to be known through the analysis of properties and functions but that, in reality, it does not belong in the details. Only the identity of the detail resides in the part, and that has to be recognized through immediate experience in order to be definitively identified. On this account, an examination of the parts of a phenomenon reveals only their physical association with one another, alike to a mechanism. Thus, the investigation of an aspect of a phenomenon does not, even by the most ingenious extrapolation, reveal the identity of the entirety. It only follows the activities of its functions.

Similarly, a living organism may be reduced to its mechanical properties, chemical composition or electrical aspects and the researcher confidently declares that biological existence is thereby understood. Achieved solely through this approach is the isolation of those properties and functions from the entirety. Thereby, biology is understood in terms of mechanics, chemistry and electricity. It might be similarly misrepresented by mathematics or, as Descartes so valiantly attempted centuries ago, the expansion and contraction of fluids.

Similarly, biological existence is not explained through the physical workings of an animal nor by the composition of its flesh and fur, and electrical activity is merely another existential explanation in electrical terms. Indeed, an understanding of biological existence rests upon none of these physical aspects. Yet, it is upon physical and calculable properties such as these that abstract rationalism manages most successfully because the intellect functions exclusively in the abstract. But to define an organism upon its physical properties and its workings is clearly insufficient because it does not explain what it actually is.

The qualitative distinction of something is indeterminable from its physical properties and the material appearance is equally misleading. But as soon as qualities are recognized an appreciation of the essential identity becomes attainable. It is not that cognitive access to the inherent quality of something is obscured but, rather, materialistic, Western philosophy has insinuated an exclusively physical approach. It requires the sole consideration of the tangible evidence, whereupon qualitative, essential distinctions are trivialized and disregarded. But, unfortunately, it is the qualitative distinction that is the intrinsic identity of something. Therefore, in order that phenomena may be correctly evaluated rationale must be recognized as merely an indirect evaluation and the object may then be immediately engaged by the human, essential identity.

Intrinsic identity is qualitative and intangible. It cannot be calculated nor deduced because its existence is essential, not superficial. There is nothing for the intellect to build upon. The intrinsic identity of a phenomenon can only be known directly and the capacity to achieve that recognition resides within the essential singularity of the human being.

Materialism would have us believe that human identity resides within the neural functions. Indeed, a brain is analyzed in order to discover its physical properties and activities. It is thought that upon the basis of the cerebral, one human being is intrinsically identified and distinguished from another. But the brain is an aspect of a compound, physical organism that functions only as the entirety. Yet, we do not attribute our identity to the heart or lungs which are similarly vital to the proper functioning of the body.

One person is intrinsically differentiated from another through the singular identity of their human existence. This is evident to immediate cognition because the human essence occupies a condition wherein extant identities are directly and experientially engaged.

Just as the essential identity of an object remains elusive to an examination of the physical condition so, also, the human intrinsicality remains undiscovered by the analytical scrutiny of our physical properties. The essential identity itself, as the quintessential authority of our human constitution, has the singular distinction of knowing that which is alike in condition to its own existence.

In summary, immediate, experiential engagement, through the aegis of the human essence occurs in a condition of immanent reality. Reality is a qualitative situation of authenticity that must be directly apprehended in order to be recognized. The immediate experience of reality reveals the authentic identity of phenomena because they are recognized for their intrinsic significance when they are known immediately. Thus, the direct experience of a thing through the singular identity of our human existence reveals its inherent condition, and through direct cognition, phenomena are discerned and identified according the intrinsic nature of the expression.

18. DIRECT ENGAGEMENT - ABSTRACT EVALUATION

The practice of direct cognition through the aegis of the singular identity of our human existence reveals phenomenal distinctions in terms of their qualitative value, intrinsic significance and essential identity. What the photographer or the painter seeks to discover and reveal is not the appearance of something nor its conventional face but that which is corporeally fleeting and would otherwise remain unnoticed.

The artist strives to bring intangible qualities to light. These are the same intrinsic significances that intrigue the observer and make an art-work meaningful. Thereupon, the artist uses expertise in a particular medium to reveal that which otherwise, would remain unknown to conventional cognition.

If the artist, having discovered something that is meaningful and authentic and, yet, materially indiscernible, were instead to attempt to describe experiential knowledge in physical terms, the materialist would easily be able to refute its existence.

The manner whereby obvious material appearances are described and the way in which knowledge concerning incorporeal realities is communicated are entirely different. They are two incommensurable cognitive methodologies that require specific practices of correspondence. Thus, the material appearance is readily described in terms of its physical obviousness and may be easily justified as authentic through its tangible properties. It can be dissected, analyzed and subjected to all the rigors of piecemeal scrutiny. Finally, declared identified and accordingly categorized, the phenomenon is considered known.

However, intangible, qualitative distinctions can only be described through metaphoric allusion because although experientially recognized they otherwise possess no physical evidence. For example, the color yellow has a qualitative distinction that distinguishes it from the color red. Experientially, that distinction is readily ascertained as authentic. That is, yellow possesses a singular, qualitative distinction that endures regardless of the context. It is known through immediate cognition to be extant, and its identity remains consistent wherever it may appear.

But upon the exclusive criterion of tangibility, a sparse perspective is extended to encompass and describe the totality of life. Indeed, it is strongly assumed by the materialist that nothing really exists without corporeal justification. That is, everything real must be tangible while all things incorporeal are considered insignificant because they are materially unjustified.

Yet, qualities are known experientially to everyone. Nevertheless, somehow we have managed to suppress our direct knowledge of them in preference for an exclusively, material understanding. Thus, we experience intangibles but determinedly construct theoretical structures and appraisals of life, that exclude them.

Qualities are assumed to be without real identity because of their intangible existence. But if they were to be suddenly removed from our experienced we would recognize the deficiency with alarm and dismay. Thereby, we recognize that the exclusively material conceptualization that we have established as an interpretation of life is entirely abstract. In fact, when considered in the light of common experience it seems ludicrous.

One wonders how a contrived and obviously prejudicial construct could come to replace the direct experience of a reality of a far greater dimension. The truth is, there never was a time when a significant population was able to differentiate between physical and essential existence. Either one or both conditions were like a dream.

Nevertheless, the modern, materialistic legerdemain has been successfully achieved through the progressively increasing authority that we have allocated to abstract evaluation, as a refutation of superstition and religious dogmatism. Even so, ironically, the two positions of materialism and religious dogmatism share much in common in that they are both ideological convictions remote from full reality. Further, indicative of the hold that a materialistic exclusivity of attention has assumed, if one were to present as authentic, directly known incorporeal realities such as the singular, qualitative existence of a color that endures regardless of physical context, the materialist would condemn the position as mere belief.

The manner whereby the materialist determines reality is almost entirely established upon the reasoning of data derived from physical properties. Thus, vast dimensions of experientially recognized existence are marginalized. The difficulty is that the existence of the intrinsic identity of immediately experienced existence is not adequately or convincingly demonstrated through dialectic. It is expressed metaphorically through art but much contemporary art hardly lives up to the challenge.

That is to say, deduction and rationalism work ideally through sequentially ordered argument in the manner of a mathematical proof. Consequently, any attempted refutation of the exclusively materialistic perspective of Western philosophy is all but impossible through argument. While abstractly conceived, materialistic, Western philosophy remains, for all intents and purposes, logically founded upon tangible evidence. Consequently, the further from material justification that knowledge of intangible, qualitative distinctions are, the less likely their authenticity may be convincingly demonstrated through rationalism.

As we have already stated, the manner whereby intangible significance is most effectively revealed may be art. But sadly, much confusion has descended in terms of that vocation. Thus, craft is readily confused with art and content has become virtually irrelevant. Diluted through confusion, art has become trivialized. Indeed, personal, psychological exorcism, the mere composition of form and color for a pleasing effect and even random hit-or-miss expression have become artistically acceptable. Therefore, today the necessary mastery of the language of the particular medium is seldom deemed prerequisite and, consequently, the once noble calling is disrespected as a means of revealing incorporeal reality and reduced to a dilettante diversion.

Yet, when incorporeal, qualitative distinctions are successfully represented, they convey immediate significance because we recognize their impressiveness and substantiveness from our own immediate, although unarticulated, experience.

We are loosely familiar with experiences of the qualitative distinctions between phenomena, but we are insufficiently schooled in isolating and expressing them. They are consequently reduced in significance. That is to say, intrinsic profundity is known experientially but incoherently communicated, and mostly denied relevance because we have preferentially adopted a materialistic interpretation of existence that is easily justified.

Yet, an accomplished artwork that reveals the authenticity of qualitative significances stirs us essentially and thereby we recognize its value. In other words, we achieve an immediate experience of something possessing qualitative importance in spite of the almost overwhelming, abstract polemic that insists upon its unimportance.

Thus, the content of an accomplished work of fine art is not experienced through sentimental evaluation. It is irrelevant whether we have a romantic or maudlin response to art because the feeling nature is dilettante and capricious and interferes with direct cognition. The significance lies in our direct experience of the authenticity of the otherwise intangible content.

However, a further distinction exists between mere experience and direct cognition whereby the latter is achieved through the auspices of the human, essential identity. Neither preconception, abstract notion, intellectual interpretation nor sentimental preference are permitted to assume authority. This is because the human essence is the ultimate significance of the human constitution. It immediately engages a phenomenon and knows it for its authenticity and intrinsic distinction.

In other words, the human essence recognizes the significance of the incorporeal content of an accomplished work of art because the extant, singular distinction is the authentic identity of the human being and it exists in an essential condition. However, this is not a belief. But it is discovered as a directly known reality when customary preconceptions, associations and interpretations are suspended. Thereby, the essence remains, and immediately recognizes itself as authentic through immediate engagement. Subsequently, the incorporeal distinction of the human being similarly recognizes and determines other intangible significances through immediate engagement.

Knowledge of this caliber is inaccessible to the conventional, cognitive approach. Only the human, essential identity has the capacity to definitively determine the existence of essential significances. While reason can abstractly justify a mathematical proof, true and false remain qualitatively incommensurable with real and unreal. This distinction reveals the difference between the working of the intellect and the evaluation of authenticity through experiential cognition.

The human essence is able to recognize the incorporeal, intrinsic identity of other phenomena, including the essential uniqueness of other human beings, because they are of a similar, essential caliber to itself. To reiterate, this situation cannot be materially authenticated because the human intellect cannot reason concerning intangible values. They must be personally and immediately explored.

However, it should be remembered that direct engagement is only a viable practice of cognition to the degree that the human, essential identity is allowed to assume an exclusive predominance and authority within the human organization. The practice of direct cognition by the human essence is much more than a mere heighten observation. Thus, essential identities remain undetermined unless upon the direct engagement of the human essence.

A notable stumbling block to the acceptance of the human, cognitive capacity of immediate engagement and of its exploration, is the manner in which the materialist summarily rejects its existence. Part of the difficulty lies in the nature of the intellect and its inability to directly recognize intangible realities and evaluate them. But the greater obstacle is the conviction that the human identity is exclusively corporeal in nature. This prejudice is extremely severe.

Nevertheless, the manner whereby the existence of the human, incorporeal essence is justified requires a direct experience of itself by itself. It cannot be otherwise known. If the individual cannot restrain the popular, materialistic conviction and for a while postpone cerebral dominance, sentimental preference and prejudice, then, direct knowledge of the authenticity of the human, conscious individuality remains elusive. Thus, the incorporeal singularity of the human being remains conceptually reduced to a material anomaly. Indeed, it may be exhaustively argued whether the incorporeal, intrinsic essence of the human being really exists as our authentic identity but ultimately everyone must explore and discover this for themselves.

However, the misidentification of the human essential with the body is a very significant error and it is worth challenging through any means. If the human essence is maligned as a mere physical organ such as the brain then direct cognition through its aegis remains unattainable since it is beyond the capacity of the brain to achieve this caliber of knowledge.

Ironically, the materialistic conviction that identifies the human, essential individuality with the body is readily confounded by simple logic. Even though it persists tenaciously, this erroneous concept remains relatively simple to refute. If the physical were indeed the determinant of human identity then a person would be someone else as a youth than when later aged. Further, the individual identity, founded upon the corporeal constitution, would alter constantly because of continuous, bodily change. Similarly, only the most strident materialist would seriously insist that two identical twins are in fact the same person.

Thus, the artificial, exclusively materialistic construct that seemed so secure is easily reduced to a mere abstraction in the light of casual examination and simple reason. Clearly, materialistic, Western philosophy is a configuration of self-deception. It is founded not upon conclusive research and exhaustive inquiry that disproves the intangible dimensions of existence but upon an abject dismissal on philosophical grounds. It is established upon the assumption that only the blatantly obvious properties of a phenomenon possess intrinsic existence. Nevertheless, careful and open-minded scrutiny of the arrangement of the entire human being would reveal a far more complex constitution than the mere, material appearance. It would be found that reference to the I or the I am, does not refer to the body or the brain but to an intrinsic individuality that is distinctive to every person. Further, the brain does not possess an intrinsic identity any more than the lung or the spleen claims singularity.

In other words the intellect only functions restrictively and selects and exclusively manages only a certain category of information that can be feasible deliberated through logic. But reason functions indirectly and can never know anything definitively except abstractly, as a mathematical postulate. It functions ideally with quantities and their relationships because it calculates and figures by nature.

The intellect functions abstractly and remotely from the event but if an objective scrutiny of the workings of the intellect continues to leave the materialist unconvinced of its constraints and limitations, materialism remains an erroneous position for another reason. That is, it contradicts the existence of intangible realities that we know personally through our own experience.

Thus, the materialistic stance misinterprets the world and our own human significance. The physical is blatantly obvious and upon superficial appearances alone we erroneously establish our identity. We reinforce this position through an exhaustive examination and categorization of material properties until it is assumed, from the sheer burden of information, that physically derived data is all there is.

But transient, material appearances belie a significant, intangible permanency. Thereby, the human, corporeality obscures the incorporeal significance that is the authentic identification of the individual.

In reality, everything has a qualitative identity that remains intangible and can only be recognized directly by the human essence. Indeed, qualitative descriptives even creep into conversation unbeknownst even to the staunchest materialist who endeavors to describe life exclusively, in material terms. In fact, life as we know it is not credible without the intangible dimension.

Nevertheless, superior, cognitive jurisdiction is assumed to belong to intellectual acuteness and to an efficiency of deduction. The intellect is held to be the supreme authority of the human constitution. Proudly, elect, intellectual authority dismiss the existence of the human, incorporeal essence as a mere belief and rejects direct cognition by the intangible identity of the human being, as insubstantial make-believe.

Yet, the irony remains that the intellectual is the one removed from reality because of the indirect functioning of abstract rationalism. The intellect will assess and evaluate, but it can never identify the existence of an object definitively because it only functions abstractly.

Thus, we have granted a monopoly of authority to a prejudiced and slanted perspective. Thereby, the incorporeal essence remains unrecognizable to the individual who insists upon an exclusively physical reality.

While modern practices of physical analysis and rational deduction are considered improved upon when compared to past centuries, in fact, materialism remains consistently stubborn and merely the manner whereby physical properties are scrutinized has become increasingly sophisticated. We simply know a great deal more concerning the physical but, through self-deception we have permitted the results of our material researches to define the entirety of existence. Thus, the exclusive arbiter concerning the constitution of reality has become our cerebral, cognitive faculty so that our perspective is prejudiced and our conclusions predictably jaundiced. Thereby, we allocate existential authenticity and merit exclusively to superficial appearances.

19. THE DISTINCTION OF THE HUMAN ESSENCE

The approach whereby incorporeal identity may be recognized and differentiated, one thing from another, is immediate. The human, essential singularity knows the incorporeal, qualitative significance of things because they are of a familiar nature to its own intrinsic existence. When the human essence directly encounters a phenomenon, it recognizes it for its qualitative distinction and overlooks the superficial, physical appearance. Furthermore, the human essence discerns the qualitative distinction as the authentic identity of a phenomenon because the approach of the human essence is direct.

Conventional cognition remains an indirect approach because it evaluates through preconceptions, abstract rationalism or sentimental preference. But intrinsic significance is an essential condition of existence that can only be discerned experientially. Therefore, indirect or abstract reasoning founded upon preconceptions cannot recognize qualitative merit as an actual things because the substantive must be immediately engaged in order to be realized.

The manner whereby cerebral and emotional assessment operate and determine the authenticity of a situation is evaluative and incommensurate with an immediate experience that determines what the primary expression of the existence of something may be. That is to say, indirect evaluation cannot discern the elemental distinction of something because a directly discerning perspective is indispensable in order to recognize integral existence. Specifically, the fundamental existence of something precedes the peripheral appearance through its profundity. Therefore, in order to be recognized it must be immediately engaged by the substantive essence that is the host of the human constitution.

Neither can a phenomenon be appraised as definitively extant upon the strength of sentimental preference or instinctual perception because of the obviously, subjective nature of discriminatory evaluation.

The manner whereby someone claims exceptional knowledge founded merely upon the conviction of the certainty of their approach is usually little more than an imaginatively conceived and emotionally sustained improvisation. A doctrine may be extensively elaborated, and supportive qualification can further ensue to persuade the convert, but there is no value in convincing oneself of the authenticity of something that is merely imagined to exist.

However, immediate engagement by the authentic identity of the human being is not a belief system or a doctrinal structure. It is a cognitive practice whereby the authentic condition of things is discovered for oneself. It rests upon the significance and nature of the authentic identity of the human being. There is nothing that needs to be believed. All that is realistically required in order to justify the existence of the human essential identity is immediate engagement. Thereafter, the direct cognition and consequent intrinsic identification of all phenomena follow as a matter of course.

Consequently, it is the human, intrinsic essence that is the benchmark of authenticity. It is through immediate engagement by the human essence that the extant condition of a phenomenon is recognized, and by its qualitative distinction its identity is determined.

The intrinsic immediacy of phenomena is a condition of existence that is only evident through direct cognition. That is, it must be experienced in order to be known. Consequently, the human, essential identity is the arbiter of authenticity because it exists in an immediately extant condition.

The one, essential absolute that we possess is the reality of our own existence. Our own definitive existence is recognized through direct engagement and we thereby establish a reference from which all other conditions may be determined for their profundity. Indeed, to the degree that existential knowledge is similarly significant the intrinsic value of something is established. Thus, it is upon the basis of the secure knowledge of the existence of the human essence that our cognition expands to encompass other phenomena and determine their intrinsic reality.

We immediately engage the authenticity of others in much the same way, and through direct experience we discern their unique identification. Therefore, dissatisfied with the excessive attention towards the superficial appearances of people and things, through the direct attention of the human essence, an unfathomed volume of significance becomes evident.

That is to say, the trivial, cursory view and the subsequent philosophical extension that represents the material surface of things is superseded by an insightful perspective that is, nevertheless, the most significant. Thus, we discover the meaningful significance of things including our own identity, through immediate experiential engagement, and once the reality of substantive existence is directly determined, we become familiar with the tenor of it.

Therefore, theoretical constructions founded upon abstract rationalism that purport to explain existence to us in the shallow terms of materialism are recognized as only indirectly inferred and not as definitive knowledge.

Definitive knowledge is understanding concerning the condition of things as they actually are. This implies pragmatically experienced circumstances that cannot be reasoned or calculated through systematic dialectic or indirect conjecture. Indeed, however grand the intellectual artifice, it will always remain a rationalistic and speculative construct in comparison to intelligence achieved through direct experience. That is, when compared with direct experience and the consequent familiarity with the condition of intrinsic significance, abstract conceptualizations, whether scientifically established or dogmatically maintained, are revealed as moot.

Upon immediately experienced knowledge of the substantive condition of things, a foundation is established that becomes the qualitative criterion for the evaluation of authenticity. That is, intrinsic existence is known as a condition wherein a phenomenon is profoundly experienced. Thus, an understanding founded upon the direct experience of the essential nature of things immediately recognizes an abstract construct that pretends to represent reality.

However, if the practice of direct cognition is considered merely from an intellectual standpoint, but remains otherwise experimentally unknown, it is of only speculative value. Furthermore, upon the remote chance that the materialist cedes value to the concept of an alternative, cognitive practice that occurs immediately, and does not dismiss it out of hand, at the most it seems merely an improved manner of observation until it is applied and authenticated through direct application. The crux of the matter, therefore, is less the viability of immediate cognition, but more significantly, the authenticity of essential existence.

Numerous philosophical constructions and belief systems exist mainly in the abstract. Their proponents insist upon the authenticity of their perspective through the strength of argument and persuasion. However, the individual, through direct cognition, confident of the tenor of reality, finds remote, intellectual abstractions at odds with reality because the authentic condition of existence has been immediately recognized and the abstract perspective is found wanting. In other words, the researcher is less persuaded by rhetoric, but more pertinently interested if immediate cognition proves the existence of an intangible volume composed of intrinsic significances.

An example may be taken from the sensational conclusions of popular, theoretical physics concerning speculation regarding alternative, physical dimensions or universes. Related to time it is thought that space may possess multiple magnitudes. However, physical dimension does not exist unless it qualifies the circumstances of a phenomenon. Therefore, abstract references regarding spatial dimension do not possess independent existence. Otherwise, it is as if we recognized the proportions of something that does not exist. Consequently, the relationship of spacial dimensions with time, as if they had significance, independent of phenomena is merely, imagined.

The abstract thinker maintains otherwise, and proportions are theoretically extrapolated as if they possessed a unique existence of their own while, in reality, they are only speculated and imaginatively endowed with independence.

Thus, a chalkboard construction of a cube is real only as a lineal representation of coordinates that, in reality, are without independent existence. That is to say, spatial conditions, isolated from phenomena are merely extracted, physical properties.

However, when an abstract projection is philosophically extrapolated and claimed to be an authentic condition of reality, we are faced with conceptual consequences that are clearly ludicrous, such as parallel universes and occasions of perpetual duplication.

It is in this sense that calculus has much in common with conventional metaphysics. Both approaches are concerned with remote, but resolutely envisioned extra-dimensionality.

However, a further proportion of significance does indeed exist beyond the physical. But the coordinates that circumscribe material conditions are incommensurate with immediate circumstances, and it within immediacy that essential significances reside.

The substantive qualification of physical conditions occupies an immanent volume. Therefore, we need not seek another physical realm because the meaningful significance of things exists intrinsically and immediately. In other words, the apparent separation between material circumstances and essential value is occasioned by an inadequate perspective, and not because we inhabit an estranged predicament of isolation.

Indeed, as we have earlier discussed, phenomena do not exist independently of their essential and intrinsic identity any more than dimensions and location possess

251

tangible independence remotely from physical phenomena.

The essential distinction between physical objects is inherent and, consequently, it must be discerned through the practice of immediate engagement that permits the discernment of intrinsic circumstances. Immediate cognition is an unconventional perspective that allows the observer to recognize the qualitative expression that epitomizes the nature of the existence of something.

Essential existence resides neither with the physical properties of phenomena nor their location in space. Further, when a phenomenon is engaged immediately, it is discovered that its intrinsic significance is unrelated to time but rather it is recognized as immanently extant.

However, contrary to the opinions of the Eastern mystical schools, the dimensions of time and space, although they do not possess independent significance, are not illusory. They exist wherever physical phenomena are apparent. It is the deception of an abstractly extended, materialistic point of view that isolates phenomenal attributes such as proportions, and bestows upon them a separate identity that does not exist.

Indeed, only the material properties are justified by materialistic, Western philosophy and they are exclusively considered the substance of phenomena. Intrinsic identities and inherent singularities remain obscure, and mention of them is treated with suspicion.

Yet, in comparison to the results of an immediate experience through the human, incorporeal, essential identity, the physical properties possesses only marginal significance because while they qualify a phenomenon, they are without independent existence.

However, this does not mean that the physical appearance does not exist but only that there would be no physical conditions without intrinsic significance. Similarly, to reiterate, dimensions and time certainly exist but, also not in a condition of independence. Thus, they cannot be extrapolated remotely from a phenomenon. To do so is to work with abstract conditions that do not possess autonomous existence, as if they were endowed with separate significance. In terms of existential reality there exists no such thing as abstract physics.

Thus, in practice, appearance is only recognized as superficial in comparison to the direct experience of the essential identity of a phenomenon, through immediate engagement. Elemental existence is recognized by the human, essential identity as of primary significance because the human essence engages the qualitative dimension of existence that is antecedent of the appearance. In this sense, if the essence of something is considered to be primary, the material state and physical coordinates must be peripheral conditions without independent existence.

Further, the intrinsic existence of a phenomenon is found to be of the same incorporeal quality as the human, intrinsic identity because both exist essentially. But incorporeality does not mean ethereal existence. It merely describes a vastly more profound condition of existence that possess absolute meaning.

In other words, qualitative significances exist intangibly, but, nevertheless, they are experientially qualified all the time. Thus, the condition in which essential qualification exists is the same dimension in which the human ipseity resides.

Conventionally, we engage phenomena indirectly, and evaluate and classify things remotely. Furthermore, the intellect rationalizes what things are and classifies them according to how they function. But, direct cognition is an entirely more profound approach because the human, essential identity directly engages the phenomenon. Thereby, it recognizes the intrinsic, qualitative distinction of the object from the perspective of its own essential condition.

The human singularity of existence is discovered to be the paramount reality of our constitution because it is not physically superficial but essentially extant. It is recognized as the significant identity of the human being and immediately and experientially known as an existential absolute. Therefore, it must be established as the foundational perspective of direct cognition.

Moving away from the conventional manner whereby we examine the physical properties of phenomena and evaluate them indirectly and abstractly in our heads, or emotionally appraise them, the practice of direct cognition concerns straightforward engagement. Indeed, the direct approach enables the human being to engage the world immanently. Thus, through direct encounter, instead of indirect evaluation, the substantive significance of things are recognized, and thereby, it is found that intrinsic existence is an absolute condition composed of immediately discerned significances.

We recognize the profound status of things directly, not merely theoretically, and consequently, we experience the authenticity of their existence. We discover that intrinsic identity is not determinable from a scrutiny of material appearances but that it exists, essentially. Therefore, compared with experientially known reality, abstractions, theoretical constructs, beliefs and imagined systems are all revealed as inadequate.

We experience essential reality through direct cognition, and consequently, we have the measure of it. That is to say, we become familiar with the profound through immediate engagement, and we know what it is like. We know the difference between immanent reality and a contrived, intellectual position because we recognize the quality and nature of elemental existence through immediate engagement. Thereby, we experience the intrinsic identity of something first-hand and acknowledge its authenticity from the perspective of our own essential person.

That is to say, our intrinsic singularity directly

apprehends the phenomenon and experiences it essentially. Thereby, we depart the concept-bound world of suppositions and theories and establish a practical knowledge of reality through a direct approach by the first-known absolute of the human constitution.

Proof of authenticity is not required because our knowledge is directly determined, not speculated, and the condition of reality is familiar to us through the immediacy of our engagement. Furthermore, the human essence is known to be authentic because it is justified experientially and qualified through direct cognition. It discerns the qualitative significance of phenomenal appearances and discovers, therein, similarly intrinsic identities alike to its own existence.

René Descartes arrived at this position but sought to qualify the existence of the experientially known reality of the human essence through reasoning. These are two incommensurate, cognitional practices. Reasoning is indirect and abstract while direct cognition is immediate and experiential. Consequently, his later, notional constructs were obscure and remote from reality.

Descartes experienced the authenticity of his own, singular existence directly but failed to conduct his further researches in like manner. Instead of immediately engaging the world from the perspective of his own essential ipseity, he questioned its existence intellectually and established a contradiction between his experiential knowledge and abstracted rationalism. In doubt, he resorted again and again to the foundational knowledge that he had experientially achieved of the absolute nature of his existence. Thus, he concluded that only his own identity and that of Divinity were definitively real.

Sadly, Descartes did not realize that the immediate manner of engagement that had allowed a direct, experiential cognition of the authentic condition of his own identity, was similarly the means whereby the intrinsic existence of all other phenomena could also be discerned. Furthermore, Descartes inadvertently revealed through his meditations the distinction between the definitive quality of knowledge achieved through direct engagement and the oblique nature of abstract deduction. Unfortunately, later generations chose to exploit merely the abstract perspective.

However, engaged immediately by the human essence, the world is revealed to be astonishingly meaningful and vivid. Everything possesses qualitative differentiation and intrinsic identity. Existence is recognized as populated with elemental distinctions with particular, essential uniqueness. Therefore, we find that the authentic, human identity, established through experiential knowledge as real, inquires beyond the superficial appearances of phenomena and discovers that which is alike to its own intransient existence. It finds everywhere, beyond the mere physical properties of objects, qualitative identities, singular and consistent, alike to its own existence.

In other words, established upon the pragmatism of immediate experience, phenomena are engaged and identified directly by the human essence and discovered in their elemental condition. Thus, the immediate, cognitional approach predominantly involves the most profound significance and essential condition of a physical situation.

However, the mystic endeavors to navigate through the incorporeal dimension of qualitative distinctions from the perspective of essential experience, with only esoteric tradition as a compass. Consequently, there is a failure to recognize and distinguish between things for their intrinsic singularity. Everything seems eternal and enlightening but remains of no practical, earthly significance because phenomena are not essentially distinguished and identified.

The essential distinction between native-element-minerals, for example, remains unknown to the mystic. But the acetic can discourse about divinity interminably. Thereby, the mystic feels alienated from the phenomenal world and becomes self-absorbed. This approach has no cognitive advantage in a practical sense because it is exclusively introvert. Indeed, we are endeavoring to discover and explore the essential identities of phenomena through a direct experiential encounter between our own authentic existence and the elemental existence of the object. Thus, our researches are established upon a practical basis. We are disinterested in experiences regarding an illusive, ethereal realm but we are eager to discover the intrinsic existence and inherent identity of phenomena through straightforward engagement.

Progress towards a significant knowledge of the intransient, incorporeal dimension of existence begins with a direct experience of the human, singular identity and is followed by the practical application of that perspective in determining the similarly essential significances of phenomena. Misinterpreted through exclusive attention allotted to physical appearances, things are otherwise, only superficially identified. But, through the direct engagement of the human essence our inquiry remains anchored and established upon a sound, directly apprehended knowledge of profound reality.

Furthermore, we approach the essential nature of existence through phenomenal appearances. But mysticism offers no such foundation. In fact, the psychic practitioner endeavors to identify incorporeal qualities and values irrespective of phenomenal evidence. Nevertheless, we recognize the essential identity of a phenomenon, but we allow that it has a material, albeit superficial, counterpart. Thus, the material circumstance is not the essential identity and, therefore, it is misleading if we imagine the appearance to be the sole distinction.

But the mystic is adrift and scarcely knows the condition of reality. Ominously, the mystic frequently denies the existence of the phenomenal world altogether and thereby erroneously confuses a temporal and superficial perspective with nonexistence.

Similarly, we recognize a significant distinction between the superficiality of an exclusively physical perspective and the intransient, essential identity of phenomena. In the same manner whereby spatial values cannot exist independently of a material condition but remain, merely an attribute or qualifier of its existence, a purely physical perspective has no value if isolated from its essential and inherent distinction.

But that does not imply that the appearance is illusory. It merely suggests that there exists a vastly more significant, intrinsic dimension than is apparent from material evidence, and that physical appearance has no existence without it. That is to say, the deficiency of the materialistic approach resides in the exclusive conferral of reality to the appearances of phenomena and their physical properties. However, through immediate cognition, the intrinsic dimension of phenomena is recognized as insufficient evidence of identity because it is without requisite, essential profundity.

That is to say, the material is a shallow view. But that does not mean that the appearance altogether has no existence. Rather, it indicates a vastly greater significance than that which merely temporal and physical evidence suggests. We do not deny physical phenomena; we experience them intrinsically through direct cognition.

Our perspective is not influenced by preconceptions, conjecture or dialectic concerning appearances as if semblances possessed an independent identity that could be qualified by abstract evidence, but through the immediate engagement of the phenomenon by the human, essential identity.

The superficial is all that can be known by conventional means, however sophisticated our reasoning and intellectual ingenuity may be. But the human, essential identity is not materially founded. It exists incorporeally. Consequently, it knows the similarly intrinsic reality of phenomena that are conventionally identified only in terms of the blatantly obvious appearances.

The error the materialist makes is in assuming that the physical appearance is the actual identity of a phenomenon. This is refuted through an immediate engagement by the human essence that reveals the existence of qualitative distinctions as the authentic identity. Therefore, intrinsicality is recognized through direct cognition that the superficial appearance that the materialist claims is the entire identity of a thing, in fact, possesses no separate, significant existence of its own.

The exploration of intangible singularities is problematic if there is no physical evidence at all. One must have a point of reference and a position of commencement; otherwise, we experience a quality but cannot identify it.

Thus, it is upon the recognition of qualitative distinctions as the authentic identity of phenomenal appearances that we establish the capacity to discern essential significances. Similarly, it is through the immediate engagement of our own essential identity, with other phenomena that we experience and know intransient reality. That is to say, we know the phenomenal world for its essential nature through the aegis of our own essence. Indeed, without the application of the perspective of our essential identity, we could only determine the superficial.

Phenomenal appearance is our foundation and essential position of inception whereby observation from the perspective of the human essence enables us to know and distinguish between incorporeal significances. Through the exploration of the intangible, qualitative distinctions that essentially comprise existence, we educate ourselves through direct engagement, and learn to identify intrinsic singularities. That is, we approach phenomena from the perspective of our own intrinsic identity and discover through immediate cognition, their essential distinctions. Further, we recognize the crucial identity of things through direct experience and further delineate their distinctions through the qualitative comparison of one significance with another. Therefore, without a phenomenal basis the attempt to fathom incorporeal identities remains a nebulous pursuit that leaves the individual uncertain because the existence of elemental reality is only surmised but not physically qualified.

The reality of an incorporeal dimension to phenomena that is of greater significance than the material appearance remains unsubstantiated without physical evidence. If the incorporeal, authentic identity is physically represented, it is known to exist. Yet, physical appearances cannot exist on their own without essential significance.

The materialist endeavors to promote the physical as the exclusive reality. But definitive knowledge of reality is achieved exclusively through immediate engagement by the human, incorporeal essence, which is the intrinsic authority of the human being. Thereby, immediate engagement reveals that the physical has no independent existence and thus, cannot be considered the intrinsic identity but that it merely qualifies the essential significance of a phenomenon.

Increasingly, we build upon directly obtained knowledge. We know of the authenticity of the human, intransient singularity because we have experienced it ourselves, directly. Through direct cognition by the human, essential individuality we know of the essential as the profound condition of existence and enter into an immediate cognitive experience concerning it.

Thus, to reiterate, an experiential examination of phenomena by the human essence recognizes the insufficiency of the merely, superficial perspective maintained artificially by the determined materialist. That is to say, we discover that the physical appearance that the materialist claims to be the authentic identity of a thing, in fact, possesses no autonomous existence. We recognize that the physical semblance is not independent of the intrinsic identity, and it is quite possible to discern essential identities as the primary evidence of elemental existence.

The human essence is the foremost authority and significance of the human constitution and, consequently, it recognizes and can distinguish between incorporeal realities that are alike to its own intrinsic nature. Indeed, it is through qualitative comparison that we learn to navigate essentially.

The abstract evaluation of physical properties is misleading because it assumes that the material appearance exists separately and isolated within itself. However, all physical circumstances occur through the impetus of a far more subtle and profound existence. To consider physical properties as if they existed autonomously is the result of determined materialism and abstract imagination but possess no foundation in experientially engaged reality.

Thus, through direct engagement we experience a qualitative dimension of existence wherein everything occurs authentically. It is not the limited perspective of the merely physical indicators and superficial appearances but one in which all things are immanently real. Through immediate experience by the human essence we engage it, fully cognizant.

Thus, we recognize the vast discrepancy between a distant, abstract interpretation of life and discernment through the perspective of the authentic, human ipseity. We experience profundity because there is nothing that separates us from it. And we discern the authentic nature of phenomena over the superficial appearance because nothing interferes with our immediate experience and subsequent, direct recognition of essentials. Thereby, we find ourselves cognizant of essentials and significances because our essential self engages them immediately.

20. IMMANENCE

A direct experience of the dimension composed of incorporeal, elemental significances reveals that immanence is unlike anything we could have abstractly conceived. We conventionally evaluate phenomena according to already established preconceptions, but the essential qualification of physical existence is difficult to imagine if we didn't already possess some inkling. In other words, although, we assume that things exist as we surmise through prior assessment, the consequences of both the oblique and the shallow view do not seem to correspond with everyday experience. It is as if a contrived explanation of existence had been grafted upon our own personal understanding through life experience.

But the authentic identity of phenomena, including our own selves and the intrinsic identity of others, can only be recognized for their definitive identity through unique experience. Unlike material appearances, the condition of essential existence is composed of autonomously significant identities. These are singularly distinct, sovereign existences. The color yellow, for example, possesses an intrinsic significance that is its unambiguous identity. As such, it cannot be represented accurately under any terms but its own particular distinction. That is to say, to describe yellow subjectively, makes a nonsense of what it actually is.

In the same vein, the essential condition of things

possesses elemental distinction and exists absolutely. But accumulated, pre-established appraisals and interpretative evaluations are the customary foundation of conventional cognition. Thereby, the established approach ensures that added information will be similarly evaluated according to prior conclusions and influenced by positions of pre-established understanding.

Needless to say, it is readily evident from an examination of our usual, cognitional practices that we must inevitably fail to definitively know the authentic identity of phenomena because we do not engage them uniquely. The conventional practice of general cognition is insufficient because we refer to our previously compiled preconceptions instead of experiencing the phenomenon originally, as an original experience.

Be that as it may, in terms of straightforward investigation, it should not be difficult to evaluate the intrinsic nature of things through direct engagement as sincerity and integrity belie the empirical method.

Direct cognition involves the immediate experience of the essential condition of phenomena. But essentiality cannot be accurately postulated because the extant state of things is only discovered and really known experientially. That is, in terms of a condition of existence, ideas pertaining to immanency inevitably remain remote because thinking is necessarily an indirect approach. Therefore, immediate cognition as a bona fide, discerning approach remains unexplored by the established research community because it is an unfamiliar and scarcely recognized methodology that is incommensurate with physicism. Simply put, a practice that supersedes rationale with insight discourages inquiry from the very beginning. Indeed, insight and discernment are not considered astute mental faculties, but they are likened to the curiosities of precognition and intuitiveness.

However, we are very familiar with rational and abstract evaluative processes and naturally imagine, thereby, that essentiality can be conceptually evaluated. But the consequences of the evaluation of incommensurate, unusual circumstances through the typical approach are depreciation and dismissal because the issue is incomprehensible from the customary view.

But the immediate engagement of a phenomenon from the perspective of the human essence requires that former associations, abstract evaluation and sentimental partiality be restrained. This means that determination through the established, cognitive procedures that we have come to rely on are overruled because they are inadequate and fail to provide definitive identification.

However, direct cognition provides a quality of intelligence that is definitive. The immediate approach allow phenomena to become known intrinsically through a straightforward engagement without evaluation, and their authentic identities cease to be obscured by previously established evaluations. Specifically, a phenomenon is essentially misidentified if it is solely considered upon the basis of its outward appearance and tangible properties. Therefore, the recognition and comprehension of intrinsic significances require an appropriate and proportionate methodology, in order to accurately determine the substantive distinction of ordinary things.

Therefore, experiencing phenomena directly and postponing our conventional manner of selective evaluation whereby we constantly compare things with our recollection of similarities, is an expedient beginning. But direct cognition alone remains an insufficient approach unless the perspective of the human ipseity is able to engage the phenomenon immediately. Yet, we cannot realistically advance from the convention of standard comprehension and suddenly begin identifying things from a unique and questionable point of view. For this reason, the usual evaluative faculties must be restrained. Thereby, by default, the human, essential identity engages an object from the perspective of its own intrinsic existence, and discovers the same fundamental distinction of other phenomena.

While the perspective of the essential human being, of necessity, remains foremost, nevertheless, direct cognition is not a subjective experience in the usual sense. The perspective of the intrinsic, human distinction is allowed immediate observational access towards circumstances when the standard, indirect approaches to understanding are postponed. In that sense direct engagement does not permit the unwarranted intrusion of personal preference, and discernment offers a thoroughly objective access quite unlike the circuitous cognitive approach.

A perspective, untrammeled by precondition and prejudice provides a uniquely direct experience of things. It is as if, for the very first time, we encounters something unknown and explores its nature without reference to pre-established concepts. An object is recognized for its unique and intrinsic value.

The ipseity is the intrinsic human identity. Indeed, by means of a simple comparison between our body and its faculties, and what we know of our existence through direct experience, the misidentification of ourselves with the biological vehicle becomes problematic. In fact, when we use the words, I am as an affirmation of our particular existence; we are describing the intrinsic identity and not the transient corporeality. Otherwise, we might attribute significant authority to any biological organ and state that I am a leg, or a head or perhaps a liver. Furthermore, if we lose some part of the body our intrinsic distinction is not reduced one iota.

The ipseity is the incorporeal singularity of human existence, and it is the perspective of our permanent existence that allows us to discern the intrinsic identity of all other things because all essential significances exist in the same condition of continuity.

The apparent contradiction that exists between the

direct experience that we have of our authentic identity and that of our physical constitution, is the same as the difference between all essential existence and superficial transience. However, as long as the human ipseity remains only an abstract concept it has little significance. Nevertheless, the consequence of the perspective of the essential person reveals the relevance of essentiality, and it is from the usage of that point of view that the existence of the ipseity is demonstrated.

When the human, essential singularity recognizes the authenticity of its own existence, the view of the ipseity becomes established as the prospective point of view of the human constitution. Thereby, we recognize the difference between the circuitous approach toward existential knowledge, and understanding through direct discernment.

Thus, the ipseity as the confirmed identity of the human being, resides as an original and enduring distinction dwelling in a context of absolutes. That is to say, the human intrinsic individual is already the sovereign authority of the human organization but at present we scarcely recognize the implication. Furthermore, in order that we become befittingly conscious of our uniqueness, whereby, we fulfill our destiny; we need to awaken to things on many levels, including, most significantly, integrity and goodwill.

Indeed, the maturation of the human being concerns the qualitative status of the soul as well as the development of existential knowledge; a subject that is treated in the later chapters of this book. But from the perspective of our incorporeal and intransient existence, phenomena can be directly engaged and definitively identified and the human being thereby achieves both cognitive autonomy and self-recognition.

In other words, the human essence alone has the capacity of discernment whereby something becomes known in the circumstances of its essential existence. Consequently, the human essence is also able to recognize the difference between real and unreal because it is, of itself, intransient, incorporeal and intrinsically authentic; in other words, fundamentally real.

Therefore, direct cognition is first applied to the human, essential identity in order to recognize the authenticity and significance of essential existence; and further employed outwardly in order to discover the profound nature of which the material appearance is an expression. Thus, the ipseity becomes consciously known for its existential significance through direct experience and it is recognized as being of vastly greater impressiveness than the former misidentification with the body.

The direct cognition of our personal identity reveals that the human, incorporeal identity is both authentic and conspicuously distinct from the corporeal constitution. It is extraordinary that we not only misidentify existence through preconceptions and

273

abstract rationalism but that we even disparage our own identity, replacing our permanence with a superficial, organic substitute. Nevertheless, the essence remains extant as the primary and authentic identity of the human being, but through the discovery of its own existence by immediate engagement it thereby becomes relevant.

The perspective of the ipseity discerns the intrinsic essential of others and physical phenomena, in the same immediate manner whereby it recognizes its own uniqueness. Furthermore, we find that the human, essential identity has a unique singularity that is without material value, and experiences its own significance to be both incorporeal and eternal in the immediate sense. Thus, human essential ipseity is found to be perpetual because it is resident in a condition of immanence and composed of intrinsic significance.

Therefore, established upon direct, experiential self-knowledge, our intrinsic and unique identity assumes its position of authority within the human constitution but it is not the body. The ipseity always resides within essential circumstances, accordingly, it is able to recognize all things similarly, essentially composed. Thus, upon awakening to the intrinsic singularity that distinguishes individual existence, it engages the world immediately and, being itself, utterly authentic it recognizes the substantial identity of all other phenomena.

That is to say, the human essence outweighs the

improper intrusion, and usurpation of the intellect, and withholds sentimental evaluation whereby it knows phenomena immediately from the perspective of its own intrinsicality. Thereby, it recognizes that the corporeal faculties are the resources of the mind, but cannot be confused with the essential distinction.

Furthermore, the dimension of existence that is engaged directly through the essence is known through the immediacy of the approach and the immanence of its existence to be entirely authentic. Thus, everything is recognized by its definitive and intrinsic identity nature. That is because the human essence only engages the profound condition of phenomena, being of a similar condition itself.

The former circumstances wherein phenomena were assessed obliquely through myriad preconceptions, accumulated associations, and evaluated abstractly or by preference, is recognized as a condition akin to blindness when compared to immediate, cognitional experience through the human, essential identity. That is to say, the intellectual faculties have become erroneously established as the supreme authority of the human being because we are ignorant of our natural precedent over the corporeal faculties.

But the manner whereby phenomena can be definitively identified is from the perspective of the essential ipseity which is both incorporeal and imperishable. Consequently, immediate cognition of

275

intrinsic significances proves the primacy of the essential person as opposed to the transient body.

The profound significance of everything is discerned through immediate engagement by the human, essential existence. Thereby, things are no longer identified by their superficial appearances and physical properties, but for their intrinsic existence. The material appearance is thought to be substantial but in reality it is superficial except in terms of the conceptual integrity that motivates its existence and functioning.

Therefore, it is a curious thing, that materialistic Western philosophy similarly denies the existence of intentional biological establishment while the most profound consideration of life is the extraordinary genius of organic origination. Indeed, the materialist seems to be content with dull happenstance and caprice in order to adequately explain viability. It is as if the academic philosopher was entirely detached from the reality and determinedly avoided even a matter of fact view of existence.

Peripheral, exclusively materialistic evidence presents an inverted perspective towards existence that can never provide definitive knowledge because it merely engages the superficial semblance of things. Conventionally, we do not seek the profound view but only recognize the apparent value of phenomena while neglecting the inherent significance. But through the immediate engagement of phenomena by the human essence, a perspective is achieved wherein existence is experienced for its significance and not merely superficially evaluated. In other words, we do not need elaborate philosophies to explain existence because we discern things as they really are.

The exercise of immediate engagement between the intrinsic identity of the human being and the world, is a unique and instant approach. Phenomena are discovered through direct cognition in their essential and authentic condition by the human essence; and directly engaged phenomena are inevitably experienced in reality because that is also the condition in which the human, essential identity exists.

The human essence, possessed of a singular and distinctive identity beyond the corporeal appearance, is discovered through direct cognition, to be virtuously composed. Thus, the authentic, human identity is revealed through immediate experience, to exist in an immaculate condition, continuously consonant with fundamental reality. Therefore, the dimension of existence, evident through cognitive immediacy, is recognized as meaningful in every respect.

Consequently, it is exhilarating to directly experience oneself and discern the authentic identities of others and phenomena. Further, when our oblique, abstract rationalism is restrained and the human essence directly engages and discovers essential conditions it is recognized that reality is an extraordinary condition wherein one finds no fault; it is a state of immanent an absolute authenticity.

The trouble lies within the vicissitudes and contradictions of the human, emotional condition wherein different degrees and permutations of fear hold sway, and the essential nature of things is obscured by ignorance.

The profound condition of phenomena, when immediately engaged by the human essence, are experienced as they exist in reality. The former, superficial perspective is recognized as remote, obscure and unreliable, and the direct consequences of the shallow view are ominous indeed.

However, interestingly the immediate experience of the intrinsic significances of phenomena as the particular distinctions that distinguish and identify one thing from another, are founded upon physical appearances. But we proceed further that the superficial and directly engage the phenomenon in order to discover its authenticity. This is possible because the human ipseity is always awake and thoroughly immediate.

Thus, mediumistic practices, trance conditions and self-induced frenzy are recognized as pointless activities for the acquisition of a definitive knowledge of reality. Revelation through occult means is of no interest to us because the human essence experiences the authentic identities of phenomena directly and consciously. The sole pursuit of knowledge is not an end in itself if the human essence remains unacknowledged. Thus the researcher must recognize that appearances are not profound but only superficial when isolated from their intrinsic significance. That being said, in reality, appearances are not illusory but merely appraised erroneously from a determined shallowness.

The Eastern mystic, for example, errs considerably in the denial of the physical because while the material appearance is indeed a peripheral perception, it is not maya, but it qualifies an otherwise essential significance. That is to say, through conventional cognition we simply do not recognize the intrinsic existence of phenomena and inevitably assume that the appearance is the entirety.

If once more we use the example of organic conceptualization, the creature itself cursorily viewed represents the superficial, but both the fact of its existence and the conceptual genius that motivates it, are profound. Thereby, we recognize the shallowness of our perspective is at fault but not the supposed illusion of the phenomenon.

It is initially a very unusual and elevating experience of wonder to recognize the authenticity of the human essence and our own singular uniqueness. When the perspective of the individual ipseity is established as the seat of cognition, others and all phenomena should be recognized for their similar significance.

The value of the greater view, however, is strongly influenced by human morality. To merely, indulge the conceit of our respective existence for its own sake is no more than egocentrism in terms of human development, and of little significant merit. Of greater importance is the recognition that everyone else is similarly, profoundly endowed and that existence is composed of intrinsic, essential identities of an equivalent caliber to our own authenticity. Thus, we keep things in perspective when self-acknowledgment is recognized to be of greater significance than mere self-indulgence.

The human essence must be consciously and directly established as the position and perspective from which all things may be engaged. The point-of-view from which phenomena are identified for their intrinsicality is, therefore contingent upon direct engagement. From a considerable foundation of essential knowledge achieved through direct cognition, all things may be sounded for the intrinsic significance of their existence.

But the self-absorbed human being, enamored through a direct experience of the incorporeal condition of existence, fails to recognize that knowledge of this caliber is not merely for personal satiation. It is the recognition of something fundamental that must be established as the predominant perspective and focal point of human consciousness. The individual must move forward from oblivious delight and recognize the profound significance of the human, essential identity as the elemental origin and destiny of the human being. Therefore, the human essence, as the intrinsic identity of the human organization, gazes outward and recognizes similar singularities in all other phenomena and distinguishes the individual identity as the distinction of all other human beings; and it becomes evident that all intrinsic identities belong to a collective reality. Each remains distinctly singular but essentially of a common existence.

This recognition assuages the possibility of self-absorption and establishes the human individuality within an appropriate context. Our singularity is acknowledged as one of the countless distinct identities that share a common kinship. Of itself, this alone is a significant experience of knowledge. Thereupon, each human being is recomposed and established with the essential identity firmly installed as the sovereign authority and, from this condition of immutability, it recognizes similarly significant and poignant entities and identities of alike incorporeal existence. Thus, every human being comes to occupy an authentic condition of existence as an integrated totality.

Essentiality is definitive, known directly, and it requires no explanation. It is autonomously extant, and it remains unmoved or deranged by our ignorance of it. It is we, ourselves, who suffer from our oblivion of that which is the legitimate condition of existence. Thus, the human essence is significant as the incorporeal and consistent identity of the human organization. It resides in an eternal condition, and it is the only aspect of our human composition to do so. Consequently, the ipseity engages a phenomenon immanently without intercession or mediation. It employs and engages itself directly and knows that which is of its own qualitative nature and, consequently, determines its intrinsic identity.

Therefore, knowledge concerning the significances that belie physical appearances is not the discovery of another separate dimension but the experience of the authentic volume of meaningful existence. Indeed, we dwell within incorporeal reality continuously. There is nowhere else. We need not indulge in the abstract fantasy of alternate universes or rarefied physical conditions of existence. But, as pragmatists, we directly encounter the reality of essential existence because we immediately engage a phenomenon and discover its authentic condition and, thereby easily differentiate the actual from the fictitious.

Conventionally, we navigate through life from lesser activities of cognition, endeavoring to discover the authentic through oblique evaluation but, inevitably, essential significances remain consistently elusive. However, through direct engagement, the intrinsic human identity engages the authentic condition of phenomena.

Accordingly, it is upon this arrangement that the human constitution is correctly reestablished in order that it may recognize and exercise existential autonomy and achieve cognitive liberty. However, lest this seems unreachable or the necessary maintenance of a conscious stance towards our own existence unmanageable and remote, it should be remembered that this is merely the reestablishment of our authentic and subsequent condition; what we are doing is waking up to it. However, with greater awareness, arises the necessity an appropriate ethos of integrity and goodwill without which the accrual of all the knowledge in the world is valueless.

21. ESSENTIAL IDENTITIES

Throughout history, and ominously even during the modern age, one way or another, under diverse pretexts an external authority endeavors to impose civil compliance with an autocratic mandate, that contradicts the ethos of cultural integrity and mutual goodwill. Formerly, the submission of self-interest in favor of the apparent better emphasis of nationalism and xenophobia may have seemed advantageous to the general populous under an erstwhile collective consciousness, but communistic allegiance even of itself no longer serves a greater good. Indeed, individual resignation to the expressed will of a human prerogative contradicts the evolutionary necessity of the successful establishment of respective principles.

Consequently, it behooves the individual to earnestly strive towards the development of a universal ideology established upon imperishable standards that exist inherently and meaningfully within the fabric not of an inferior indecent nature, but upstanding civility.

However, the only apparent way whereby one can be certain whether an ideological concept exists intrinsically and not merely as an innovative product of human conception, is through the direct cognitive approach; whereby, it is possible to become familiar with the timbre of substantive existence.

For example, the immediate experience of our

own, intrinsic distinction permits the establishment of the human ipseity as our predominant perspective whereby all other phenomena may be correspondingly evaluated. Thereupon, the exclusively material condition of things is instantly discovered to be an inadequate representation because it appears too shallow. In fact, we will find that a qualitative existential dimension is lacking from the merely physical definition.

However, the perspective of the human essential ipseity is difficult to establish because the mind does not willingly relinquish the customary authority of the arbiter of all things pertaining to adjudication. Consequently, the more effective approach is less a forcible change of overview but the temporary restraint of accustomed evaluation through the introduction of an open and receptive state on mind. Thereby, upon a studied moderation of rationale, partiality and pre-conceptual conviction, we inevitably find that the human essential distinction becomes the foremost perspective.

From the straightforward perspective of our own intrinsic identity the qualitative significances of phenomena become evident. That is to say, through immediate engagement, we discover the definitive nature that intrinsically differentiates one thing from another and thereby discern the particular manner of their expression. In other words, we discover the profundity of the existence of things.

Needless to say, accustomed to abstract

assessment and intellectual evaluation founded upon preconceptions and preferences, we find ourselves overwhelmed when we experience something directly and definitively identify it for its qualitative distinction. Even the direct experience of our own particularity and the realization of our singular uniqueness is breathtaking. Furthermore, it is wonderful to experience the incorporeal dimension of intrinsic existence because in an essential way, all of a sudden, we recognize a wealth of fundamental relevance that, formerly, we failed to notice. In that sense, we find that essential circumstances are substantively meaningful, and through the immediacy of our approach, of greater significance than the mundane physical appearance.

In the same manner whereby we directly experience the authenticity of the singular distinction of our own existence so, also, the human essence discovers the authentic, essential identity of all other phenomena. This includes the intrinsic significance of other people. That is to say, the human, essence recognizes the original distinction of others through direct cognition and finds the individual, essential identity to be qualitatively beyond reproach; although the dispositional character is another thing.

In this way, we discover through our own direct experience, that the physical circumstances belie the intrinsic distinction of something. Furthermore, the discernment of the essential condition reveals that the substantive is recognizable not through some esoteric endowment but merely upon the exercise of immediate cognition.

Gratefully, in this sense, the meaningful volume of a phenomenon is identified when conventional cognition is delayed in order that a direct engagement between the individual self-hood and the object may be accomplished without interference. In other words, the direct approach refers to an immediate experience whereby the human essential ipseity discovers the similarly imperative existence of another entity. Expressed differently, when something is engaged without abstract reflection or sentimental preference, it can be recognized upon the condition of its elemental existence.

The identification of incorporeal realities is beyond the scope of the intellect because cerebral calculation and evaluation are necessarily indirect approaches. When reason attempts to challenge or justify the existence of intangible realities it finds it can only allude to them, one way or another, through implication. Consequently, argument is an insufficient means of justification because it convinces but it cannot definitively demonstrate the existence of something except through the justification of extracted, quantifiable information.

The fact that the intellect functions most expediently through calculation cannot be overemphasized. In other words, rationale does not arrive at an unequivocal conclusion unless the data that it handles is of an accountable nature. Consequently, the mind must estimate in order to resolve a disparity if the evidence is unsuitable to enumeration, and appraise a problem in a reasonable manner without being entirely certain if the solution is true.

Not surprisingly, verification of the existence of the ipseity as the incorporeal distinction of the human being, is similarly beyond the scope of scientific methodology. In that case, definitive evaluation is impractical particularly when we are concerned not with computation but whether something is real or not.

However, those things that are without physical substance are not necessarily materially unrepresented. Indeed, intrinsic significance is consistently implied by the fact of manifest concurrence. Put another way, it is only through the evidence of material existence that the intrinsic significance of a phenomenon can be discerned. However, if the obvious condition of something did not lead the openminded researcher towards the greater profundity of its existence, then for all intents and purposes, as far as the human being is concerned, the postulate concerning deeper relevance would be unsupportable.

Against this background, we must discover an approach whereby the material circumstances that are considered the exclusive manifestation of a thing, are shown to belie a greater connotation. With this in view, clearly it is the narrow, abstract preoccupation of the researcher that prevents the discovery of intrinsic knowledge. Or to put the matter another way, the distraction of speculative thinking concerning a phenomenon, prevents a deeper understanding because we already dismiss metaphysical evidence as unreliable. Thereafter, only the physical is deemed pertinent.

A more significant hindrance concerns the extension and elaboration of the consequences of an oversimplified understanding of existence into existential philosophy in order to reduce the discrepancy between physically verified knowledge and unresolved issues. In this way, we endeavor to arrange our ideas to fit the facts and simultaneously to explain the unknown.

Naturally, there is an approach whereby the profundity of existence becomes readily discernible. But it is through a lack of understanding of the straightforward cognitive approach that the materialistic view imparts a purposeless and banal opinion towards existence. Indeed, it seems as if circumstances entirely depended upon electrically charged minutiae; a conviction that is the direct consequence of a persistently oblique study of the mechanical properties of things.

In order to discover the intrinsic merit of physical circumstances, it is necessary to allow phenomena to speak for themselves. However, in order to be directly discern the meaningful significance of something, we cannot proceed while simultaneously continuing to maintain a mechanical or physical partiality. That is to say, we must diminish those practices that obstruct the profound view, and attend to the qualitative expression that epitomizes what something intrinsically is. Thus, while the physical serves to focus our attention because otherwise we would be unable to differentiate between particular natures, nevertheless, the significance of the discovery of essential circumstances is of a profound importance that extends far beyond the shallow view.

If one inquires why it remains unclear that a purely physical or even chemical focus produces a similarly technically specific philosophy, we must look most closely at the phenomenon of specialization. In our modern time, the world is increasingly populated by academic specialists. But, depending on the depth of the forte, we establish exceptional knowledge in one area often at the expense of the overview. This situation potentially gives rise to abstract thinking concerning other circumstances whereby the intricacies of a very narrow perspective are contrived to extend beyond the area of expertise.

Hence, it should be of no surprise that the scientific investigator of the heredity genotype would establish and extend an understanding of existence based upon the findings of an incredibly narrow branch of biology. In the same way, the astrophysicist from an extrinsic perspective might also claim an exclusive point of view. In the meantime, the unsophisticated person would be hard pressed to make sense of either philosophical approach particularly as the existential convictions of the specialist appears to contradict commonsensible wisdom.

Fortunately, the way forward towards a meaningful understanding of life does not require specialism nor particular scientific training because neither approach brings us any closer to the recognition of substantive significances. Indeed, academic specialization is incommensurate with our inquiry into intrinsic circumstances if it remains solely concerned with the technicalities of matter and material organization.

It is important to remember that the human being resides at present in a condition of existential limbo. In fact, generally speaking, most of us remain confused concerning our manifest circumstances and greater objective, while philosophy serves little towards a meaningful reorientation. Indeed, the doctrine of an exclusively material existence, isolated from realistic rhyme and reason works against human improvement except to the degree that it provokes the investigation of a sensible replacement.

Accordingly, it is important and increasingly crucial to human survival that we each reassess our priorities. With this in mind, we turn our attention towards the profound and relinquish the banal and superficial. Thereupon, sooner or later depending upon our sincerity, we discover that there exists an intrinsically meaningful proportion to existence that underlies the appearance of things and wherein resides the significance of phenomena. We affirm this not through conviction or belief but because the immanent volume of material circumstances may be individually discovered as extant through immediate cognition.

The human essence recognizes itself experientially and immediately. Thereby, the essential identities of others and the intrinsic nature of phenomena become definitively discernible through direct cognition. That is to say, the human essence is experientially knowledgeable concerning its own authenticity and it discovers the identities of phenomena because of a similar, qualitative distinction of identity.

Essential identities are of an analogous caliber through their profundity but remain intrinsically distinct on the basis of respective qualitative expression and particular distinction. Thus, we recognize that direct cognition is pragmatic because it engages the physical appearance of a phenomenon but, through the aegis of the authentic, human distinction, it additionally discovers the qualitative dimension and essential significance that is the meaningful proportion of things.

The distinctions of singularity, of identity and individuation are the incorporeal relevances that underlie physical dimensions and properties. Thus, while phenomena exhibit a three dimensional existence, the significance exists qualitatively and possess intrinsic identity beyond their physical appearances. Furthermore, it is the essential, qualitative identity of the entirety that distinguishes and separates one thing from another.

Although the coordinates of material appearances represent physical positions in time and space, they cannot exist in isolation from the essential identity. Nevertheless, we have become exclusively preoccupied with physical circumstances while overlooking the essential condition which is the actual distinction. However, through immediate cognition we soon begin to recognize that our authentic identity occupies an intangible volume wherein individual significance, as the distinction between phenomena, is the navigational foundation whereby entities are distinguishable. Therefore, the direct experience of our own incorporeal distinction and that of other human beings, lead us to the discovery that the incorporeal dimension is independently populated by intrinsically singular identities.

The circumstances of intrinsic existence is without physical parameters. This is an extraordinary realization particularly from an almost exclusively material perspective. Consequently, we may imagine that immediacy is of lesser significance than physical existence and mistake the superficial with the substantive. In reality, the volume of immediacy that qualifies physical circumstances with meaningfulness, is of vastly profounder relevance than the appearance. For this reason it is important that we try these things for ourselves because conviction is negligible compared to immediately ascertained knowledge.

Put differently, the superficial three-dimensional appearance of someone is obvious, but the essential person exists immanently and is discerned from the profound perspective of our own substantive existence. Yet, we are alone in our singularity, and this enables us to recognize the uniqueness of other entities. Thereby, through immediate cognition, perhaps unawares we enter incorporeal space and a dimension whose coordinates are essentially qualitative and intrinsic.

That is to say, the immanent volume is without quantifiable proportions, yet identities are differentiated through the qualitative expression of their existence. However, the singularity of the essential existence of ourselves allows us to maintain our own autonomy and distinguish between phenomena on the basis of their intrinsic uniqueness.

The essential, unique distinction of a phenomenon is only discovered through an immediate encounter between our own essential person and that of the object. But qualitative distinctions, while incorporeally relevant, are neither mysterious nor inexplicable. Yet, from the materialistic perspective, a quality appears to be merely an aspect of the physical, without intrinsic significance. Nevertheless, qualitative distinctions possess an independent uniqueness of identity which describes the intangible dimension of a phenomenon in a manner inaccessible through physical evaluation.

However, a discrepancy exists between the capacity of perception accessible to our human, intrinsic identity and that of our rational and feeling-sentient cognitive faculties. But the human singular essence is the profoundest authority of the human being and possesses the capability of discovering definitive existential knowledge. However, while the human essence remains in a constant condition, the intellect offers only indeterminate results and the feeling nature of the human being can be quixotic, mercurial and readily disturbed. Indeed, the feeling-sentient nature of the human constitution is readily thrown about like a small boat upon the ocean because of its intimacy with the corporeal condition and isolation from the constancy of the human essence.

Therefore, discovering one's own authentic identity through experiential cognition and recognizing the significance of things for ourselves, as they in fact exist, provides a formidable cognitive foundation whereby the human, feeling nature becomes profoundly impressed. Thus, the recognition of the human, individual essence, the authentic identity of others and a direct knowledge of the essential identities of phenomena, beneficially influence the emotional aspect of our constitution. They offer a nourishing and stabilizing effect because they assuage existential anxiety.

An abstract evaluation of life in terms of physical appearances provides little substantial assurance, addressing as it does, only the superficial aspects of phenomena and it leaves the soul bereft. Therefore, life represented exclusively in superficial terms, can be existentially alarming. Similarly, confidence in an unsubstantiated belief system that must be constantly reinforced through allegiance to a particular dogma, offers only dubious solace. But direct, experiential cognition through straightforward engagement provides a sureness of footing that increases with familiarity.

22. VIRTUE

The color yellow possesses intrinsic significance that remains consistent regardless of where the color may appear. Yellow is a qualitative reality without physical form although it exists physically as a qualifier to material conditions. However, the intrinsic existence of the essential identity of the phenomenal color yellow is not conditional upon physical circumstances, but it exists irrespectively of the material context. The authentic identity of the human being is similarly, intrinsically extant.

The dimension of immanent existence, unlike material semblance, possesses no physical coordinates. Every essential value is engaged immediately and distinguished for its inherent distinction of identity. Thus, the intrinsic significance of yellow is found immediately and, consequently, it is discernible for its extant identity through direct engagement by the similarly immanent, human essence.

Virtue is of an essential, elusive quality similar to intrinsic significance, and it ennobles the human being. It exists in an essential, intrinsic condition and is approached immediately because it too, is without physical correspondence.

However, the human soul approaches incorporeal existence differently from the human, essential identity. The human essence is already justified as authentic through immediate experience and engages intrinsic circumstances immediately. But the soul must engage through sincerity and open-heartedness. Furthermore, the soul reaches for succor without the advantage of definite knowledge. It is ignorant of the identity of Virtue and consequently, Virtue must be permitted to be entirely as it is. This is the true meaning of the biblical directive of dispositional faith.

In other words, faith is not imagining that something miraculous will occur if we believe sufficiently and convincingly. That is magic. Faith is a condition of sincerity and an admission of ignorance, whereby Virtue may become known for what it is authentically, or not at all.

Virtue is engaged immediately through the heart. When the soul approaches Virtue it finds that it corresponds constitutionally but that the inner nature is not of the same qualitative condition. The human soul, however, becomes virtuously reestablished through the influence of Virtue.

We engage a phenomenon immediately recognizing that its physical appearance is peripheral and superficial. Our incorporeal existence is able to discern its qualitative dimension and thereby identify its intrinsic significance.

In terms of Virtue, we recognize that it does not possess a physical semblance, and it is not corporeally justified. We have no point of departure from where we can penetrate to its authentic existence. Yet, we do not wish to imagine and characterize Virtue or endeavor to fashion it to conform to our desire or established opinion. This is both pointless and delusional, and much like the unsatisfactory conventional, cognitive approach that we are trying to supersede.

Knowing experientially, through direct cognition, the immanent nature of the incorporeal dimension, we recognize that Virtue is already of impending significance. If Virtue is to be approached authentically, it must be experientially engaged, open-heartedly by the soul, without preconception or precondition. Indeed, we would not wish Virtue to be anything other than it really is and certainly not as we imagine. We are determined to learn of Virtue solely through immediate engagement and direct experience, but it is the soul that requires reconstitution and not the essential identity. Thus, it is the heart that must open to Virtue in order that the human psyche may become qualitative refashioned.

If we already possessed Virtue in the manner required for a significant future and for the unfolding of our destiny we could reconstitute our own feeling-sentient nature. But we do not possess it and we must consequently allow it to be extrinsically introduced.

Thus, the way of sincerity and of open-heartedness, together with a willingness to allow Virtue to refashion our feeling sentient nature, is an authentic achievement of direct engagement through a different approach. The reality of Virtue becomes known to us immediately, and its subsequent influence upon the soul is not ours to decree. The authentic nature of Virtue will be as it is in reality and that is our only persuasion. Thus, we come to know the reality and qualitative singularity of Virtue cumulatively through our own direct experience. But sincerity and open-heartedness remain our only condition of approach because otherwise the psyche remains inaccessible.

Similarly to our engagement of phenomena through direct cognition whereby we determined the essential significance of things, we approach virtue actively, recognizing that what we are doing is enormously significant. Yet, it is neither a superstition nor a diversion. We are opening our innermost condition of soul to Virtue with the explicit intention of allowing Virtue to reconstitute our psyche.

Virtue establishes a new and confident morality within our feeling-sentient constitution that is far removed from self-righteousness and puritanism. It is the morality of maturity and dignity. It is remote from piousness and fanaticism but established upon the magnitude of experiential empathy, respect and goodwill.

We have already recognized that abstract rationalism deals remotely and obliquely and fails to determine the existence of intrinsic significances. Nevertheless, the intrinsic individuation of an entity is only known experientially. It therefore behooves us to allow the significance of Virtue to remain as it is without our interference or misinterpretation. We will otherwise only harbor a distorted conception. It is sufficient that our hearts are actively open to the transforming influence of Virtue, particularly during specific moments of need when we are challenged and recognize dispositional inadequacy.

The exploration, in a former chapter of the distinctions between native-element-minerals, enabled us to recognize their qualitative identity and to differentiate between them based upon their intrinsic significances rather than mere appearances. The qualitative singularity of each became known to us to the degree that we permitted ourselves to uninhibitedly experience them uniquely. We did not sully a direct engagement with theories, preconceptions or details concerning their physical properties. It was the intrinsic distinctions that interested us. In other words, in order to experientially discover essential identities, it is essential to engage phenomena, originally.

We adopt a similar attitude when we approach the qualitative individuation of immanent Virtue. We allow the influence of goodness to restructure our psyche without restricting grace to the limited definition and meager understanding of our present condition of perception.

In much the same way that we abstractly evaluate and define phenomenon through logical evaluation, pursue a belief system or allow our sentimental assessment to cloud our perspective, Virtue is misidentified if we endeavor to predetermine its identity and nature. Without preconception, we engage Virtue as it is, however that may be, through sincerity and open-heartedness. Virtue must not be abstractly misconstrued as something else while remaining under the same name. It must be permitted to remain as it is and not be distorted according to our preconceptions. Otherwise, we merely entertain a fantasy of our own construction.

It is not only desirable to approach Virtue without misconstrual but essential. If we imagine Virtue to possess qualities of our own devising, we remain in the position of the practitioners of magic and superstition that attribute supernatural powers of their own choosing to a deity of their own fabrication. An immediate experience of Virtue reveals its authentic existence and its distinction is experienced as an inherent singularity in the same manner whereby we recognize and distinguish any incorporeal phenomena. Keeping these things close to us, in our hearts, is an aspect of the reestablishment of our feeling sentient nature, through sincerity.

It is not necessary to define Virtue but we approach it sincerely and consequently, we know it experientially by qualitative distinction. Similarly, sincerity is the prerequisite condition of soul. Sincerity is not a technique or a practice. It is either certain or it is not.

Virtue is also permitted to be as it is and to

influence the soul appropriately for the present reorientation of the psyche and our future, wholesome development. We did not fashion ourselves, and our destiny is similarly ordained and ensued by other hands. Our choice is to continue or prevaricate. That is to say, our task it to facilitate the ingression and transformative influence with sincerity and an open heart. Thus, faith, in the manner presented above, is important to an immediate experience of Virtue, as is sincerity and open-heartedness without any distortion or precondition whatsoever.

The reestablishment of the soul through the direct influence of Virtue engenders a condition of authentic morality through the aegis of an exemplary nature. In other words, we establish within the human heart a successive nature, through sincere receptivity.

Virtue, alike to any phenomenon that one engages directly in order to discover its authentic identity, must be experienced immediately, without assessment, in order that it may be recognized as it really is. The entire significance of direct cognition resides in the immediate approach, avoiding evaluation through abstract rationalism, sentimental preference or imaginative misinterpretation. It is the same way with respect to openhearted sincerity.

That is to say, through immediate cognition, a phenomenon is experienced directly, and through openhearted sincerity Virtue is also straightforwardly

305

engaged and its influence unequivocally accommodated within the soul.

In the same manner whereby a color is recognized for the particular distinction that identifies it and distinguishes it from other colors, Virtue is approached without preconception in order that it may be experientially known for what it authentically is. Similarly, this is the joy of openhearted sincerity. The human soul surrenders resistance in complete confidence when once the exemplary nature is personally experienced.

Virtue is engaged directly and discovered as it is in reality. It is encountered through sincerity which is the way of direct cognition, and endorsed open-heartedly. This is of far greater significance and profundity than imaginative evaluation whereby attributes are assumed that are false and inappropriate, while other more essential values are dismissed through misconception.

Far better that we recognize the authentic condition of any entity or phenomenon than we construct an edifice that bears no resemblance to the original. Therefore, we must allow things to be as they really are.

Typically, we establish pre-conceptual evaluation and assessment to everything that we encounter. Nothing, not even our own identity, is recognized for what it is authentically. Indeed, unless the essential identity of the human being engages a phenomenon immediately, and without interference, allowing it to remain what it intrinsically is, definitive knowledge of intrinsic significances remains elusive.

If we continue, accustomed as we are to cerebral evaluation, conceptualization and the influence of preference as our characteristic manner of cognition, we maintained an interpretation of the world that is remote from reality. Indeed, without direct cognition through the expedience of the human, essential identity, we merely exchange one appraisal for another and fail to escape our abstracted and prejudiced position. Thus we can never know things as they are in reality.

Nevertheless, we possess the inherent capacity to recognize phenomena for their intrinsic identities through direct encounter. Everything is engaged immediately without prejudice. Another human being is no longer evaluated for their transient condition or superficial appearance but recognized for their intrinsic identity through the perspective of our own inherent singularity. In much the same way as phenomena can be immediately experienced and discovered for their authentic existence, Virtue must be similarly engaged without preconception in order that we are not misled into imagining that Virtue is something other than what it is.

23. INCORPOREAL UNIQUENESS

The human, essential identity comes to the fore as the sovereign cognitive authority when intellectual abstraction, preoccupation with established belief systems, contrived constructions and sentimental preferences are set aside.

René Descartes demonstrated through abstract rationalism that no proof is possible as to existence of physical phenomena if doubt is raised concerning the authenticity of evidence garnished solely through the human senses. Through elaborate abstraction, he even doubted the validity of experientially attained knowledge regarding his own existence. He was thereby thrown into an existential quandary because he failed to distinguish between rationalism and immediate, experiential cognition. By this means Descartes demonstrated not only the fallibility of physical sense-information but the inadequacy of the intellect to definitively determine authenticity.

Direct engagement is a cognitive approach that involves an entirely different dynamic from reasoned exposition. Therefore, through an immediate engagement between the human essence and a phenomenon, existential intelligence becomes experientially evident. It matters little what the quality of sense-information is because it is not the physical appearance that we are interested in. We acknowledge the peripheral representation but only as a material condition that belies the significant identity. But we wish to know the essential identity of a thing and not merely its superficial appearance. The senses reveal information concerning the appearance but the human essence directly discerns that which is intrinsically significant.

Descartes discovered the authenticity of his own existence through direct engagement while, through reason, he discounted the significance of sense-information and concluded that the existence of corporeality was beyond the capacity of reason to confirm.

Materialistic, Western philosophy continues to include existential doubt as a valid perspective towards life, rationalizing profusely while simultaneously recognizing that reliance upon reason alone is an inadequate means of definitively determining authenticity. Thus, the centuries old theoretical debate continues concerning the validity of sense-information while, in fact, sense reliability is only abstractly significant and scarcely matters in terms of the immediate engagement of phenomena for their essential significance.

When a phenomenon is immediately engaged, the senses serve merely to establish a focus. But the human, essential identity does not rely on sense information in order to determine the innate existence of something or to evaluate what it is. It recognizes the intrinsic significance, which does not reside with the physical condition. Thus, Descartes inadvertently demonstrated the inability of sense information alone to determine the essential significance of something, to the comparable and qualitative extent that he had immediately experienced his own existence.

Descartes discovered the authenticity of his unique singular identity, not through reason or through the evidence of the senses, but experientially. Indeed, the human essence is intangible and can only be determined through immediate encounter. The manner whereby phenomena are recognized for their intrinsic, intangible significance, is direct engagement through the human essence. Reason is insufficient to the task.

Direct cognition is a practice of discernment by means of which the human essence engages phenomena and discovers their actual identity. It is an immediate approach whereby the real identity of the individual engages a phenomenon and identifies its intrinsic existence.

The human essence exists incorporeally and it is, consequently, able to discern the similarly intangible, essential identity of other phenomena. Thus, the distinction between appearance and the essential identity of phenomena is readily accessible through an immediate encounter by the human, essential singularity. The appearance is the transient and superficial proportion that cannot exist without the essential significance of a phenomenon.

Similarly, a discrepancy exists between the immaculate nature of the human essential significance and the condition of the feeling sentient nature. Thus, the prevalent condition of the human soul is our heritage while the substantive conditions that we experience through the aegis of our essential singularity, is our destiny.

Lest the turning of the soul towards Virtue would seem slight and of marginal significance, it should be intoned that the soul consists of an individual and collective psychic condition whose disorder is the recognized culprit of considerable, human malaise. There is no future of any significant unless this condition is addressed.

Through sincerity and open-heartedness, the principle of Virtue is immediately experienced by the soul. Thereby, the human soul is reestablished through direct influence to the degree that we are sincere in our approach and willing for our mentality to be appropriately refurbished in a manner requisite to a meaningful future.

Virtue reorientates the soul and steadily diminishes the no-longer viable mentality of the past that persist in various guises and combinations of apprehension. Through soul transformation, our destiny is assured. But without the direct influence of Virtue upon the soul and its consequent renewal, everything else is in vain. Thus, it is very timely that we take this to heart and explore it with the utmost sincerity and diligence, and that we do so authentically, without attempting to reconfigure Virtue according to a concept of our own imagination.

Indicative of a significant flaw in human understanding, is the religious practice whereby an attempt is undertaken to use Virtue towards a particular end, as if it were a nondescript energy or something that can be coaxed into service to our advantage. Often, it is erroneously imagined that when certain sequential rituals are performed an anticipated result will ensue. This is merely traditional magic and superstitious custom in a contemporary guise. In a similar but more sophisticated vein and one less magical in appearance, the practitioner, on the strength of a determined faith and trust, forcefully imagines that the desired result will be inevitably forthcoming. Thus, the consequence of blind conviction is imagined to be a miraculous reward. The follower of this approach claims justification upon the strength of the many wonders attributed to this technique. However, upon closer scrutiny, it is discovered that most of the consequences attributed to the cause-and-effect approach are circumstantial and not inviolable.

Alternatively, it is imagined that through training and discipline the significance of the human soul may become marginalized. Both the Eastern devotee and the monastic disciple of the West have traditionally struggled

313

through ascetic discipline and rigorous self-abnegation in the attempt is to overrule the inadequacies of the soul through renunciation. This toilsome and dogged struggle brings to mind the biblical reference of taking of the kingdom of heaven by storm.

Conversely, the hedonist pursues all manner of diversion, confident of the fallacy of the ascetic approach and unconvinced of any negative consequences to self-indulgence. This position, similarly to that of the renunciate, rests upon an ignorance of the necessity and immanent availability of a renewal of the human soul, in order to achieve a meaningful destiny.

The soul is the respective psyche and it cannot be renounced. It must be reestablished and renewed in a manner suitable to a meaningful future. We ensoul the past, but our future advancement requires a different demeanor. In order that the soul may be restored upon an appropriate footing suitable to a worthwhile future, it must be open to the direct influence of Virtue. This is not achieved through ritualistic repetition, austerity or arcane superstitious practice. It cannot be forced through human will-power or conviction. It merely requires an immediacy of approach, sincerity and open-heartedness. The rest is not in our hands and indeed, it cannot be.

We currently have a cumulative condition of soul that has no significant future. What we require in order to attain our full potential and consequent destiny, is a caliber of morality that we do not yet possess. To the degree that the soul is reestablished through the corrective and restorative influence of the principle of Virtue, the authentic identity of the human constitution is able to come to the fore as the undisputed authority. The psyche is no longer an impediment and a distraction but it is elevated, qualitatively alike to the human essence. Consequently, the entire human constitution is reestablished to work in concert.

Thus, the authentic identity of human individuation and the renewed soul come to the fore in a condition of unification. Intrinsic significances become known through direct engagement and the human organization moves from oblique cognition to an immediate experience of how things profoundly exist. Simultaneously, a reestablished feeling sentient nature adds a further qualitative dimension.

We are again addressing the immediate experience of intrinsic existence. We have established that direct cognition is a justified faculty of the human constitution whereby the condition of reality may be immediately and experientially known. Indeed, contrived systems and make-believe of any caliber are abhorrent to the human essence. We desire to know things for what they are of themselves and to know their authentic identities and we are ill content with anything less. Virtue is similarly approached without presumption or preconception.

Only the authentic identity of the human

constitution, the incorporeal identity, can know substantive conditions directly. The ipseity is itself essential and consequently it only acknowledges the profound. No lesser, corporeal aspect of the human being has this capacity. Furthermore, it is senseless to imagine that we have understanding or control over Virtue. In fact, we scarcely know the difference between real and unreal. Therefore, the soul must defer to Virtue with an appropriate attitude of trust.

The human, essential singularity observes phenomena from the secure perspective of directly experienced and known astuteness. That position is founded upon an immediate knowledge by the human essence of its own unique authenticity. The human constitution is thereby established upon an absolute and directly recognized, elemental condition. There is nothing of greater significance within the human make-up than the conscious singularity which is our incorporeal existence. Therefore, recognizing the significance of our own intangible identity, the existence of Virtue is similarly, experientially discovered to be authentic.

The significance of immediate cognition by the human ipseity and the reason why direct cognition is an autonomous experience of knowledge, lies in the fact that we primarily exist quintessentially.

Therefore, Virtue is necessarily, directly approached. It is engaged with an attitude of deference, because we give it ready access to our feeling sentient nature. We know that in order for our feeling-sentient nature to be transformed it must be reconstituted in a condition of vulnerability towards the ingress of principle. This seemingly unpleasant state of contrition is not self-righteousness or debasement. It is willingness, susceptibility and sincerity. We know the tenor of reality through direct cognition and we desire our association with Virtue to be on the same terms of authenticity.

Any approach that is structured or formulaically conceived will be inevitably contrived. If we desire authenticity then our manner must be sincere. If it is our unfeigned desire that Virtue restructure our feeling sentient condition in order that we may enjoy both a wholesome present and a worthwhile future, then we must allow Virtue access to our hearts. Sincerity and open-heartedness are not the prerequisites of a methodology or practice they are the authentic condition of soul whereby Virtue may, in reality, rearrange our innermost disposition.

In the animal kingdom the disposition of a creature is altered through its response to ecological challenge. The adjusted temperament alters the form because the nature of the creature is changed. A change in nature induces alterations of appearance.

Similarly, the condition and constitution of the human soul is cumulatively etched upon the appearance. Of greater significance, an unproductive predisposition wreaks havoc upon our entire mental and emotional health. Indeed, a propensity towards detrimental conduct becomes increasingly tenacious with habit, souring our existence, and neither is it dislodged by the force of our will.

To our advantage or liability, every human being has a heritage of pre-established proclivities. There is very little essential liberty possible when we find ourselves predestined in this manner. In anticipation of a future that promises a thorough latitude of autonomy, it remains critical to us to dispense with our unproductive and entrenched temperaments. This is unachievable by means of willpower or wishful thinking but available through willingness. It is remarkably uncomplicated requiring only that the human soul make itself accessible to Virtue.

24. THE UNIQUE HUMAN BEING

It is possible to recognize a person who we know well, from a considerable distance through subtle indications and not merely by their stance or manner of movement. Indeed, two portraits of the same person by different artists are never alike yet, both may be recognized as good likenesses. That which the painter strives to capture and articulate is the essential identity of the subject which is independent of physics and circumstances. Consequently, different perspectives will portray alternative aspects of the quintessential identity striving to articulate the essence that is otherwise not materially represented.

Essential identities such as the singularity of a person revealed astutely through portraiture or the intrinsic character of an animal discovered by observing the characteristic demeanor in relation to a particular ecology, are not revealed merely by describing their obvious, physical properties. The intrinsic identity is known through direct discernment. However, this is not just a condition of heightened sensibility, but it involves an engagement that is much more profound. Indeed, in order to reveal the intrinsic significance of a subject through a portrait or sculpture, the artist must directly discover the authentic identity.

The human being possesses an incorporeal consequence that is unlike the physical appearance

319

because it is individually characteristic. It is this quintessence that the master, portrait artist endeavors to determine and describe.

Not content with a mere physical and superficial appraisal; we wish to discern essential identities. But that requires direct engagement by our own intrinsic identity. It requires that the quintessence of the human constitution encounter the phenomenon immediately and thereby discover the intrinsic permanence and essential significance of the object. This is direct cognition.

Immediate cognition necessitates that the authentic identity of the human being engage a thing straightforwardly. Thereby, the direct approach requires the establishment of a perspective through our own absolute identity, in order to recognize intrinsic significances without subjective distortion.

Direct cognition is a legitimate faculty of the human constitution that is merely obscured by an almost exclusively abstract and frequently sentimental, preoccupation. Direct cognition is so unlike our conventional and superficial approach that it has become clothed in obscurity. Where acknowledged at all by materialistic, Western philosophy it is marginalized as arcane and mysterious.

The stumbling block to a wholehearted acceptance of the significance of direct cognition lies in the misidentification of the human quintessence, with the body. Yet, it becomes evident upon immediate, experiential introspection that the human, conscious distinction is indeed incorporeal and of conspicuous singularity.

Direct engagement requires the meeting of the human, authentic identity with the object of inquiry but it occurs inevitably when the noisy machinations of the intellect and our intrusive sentimental preferences are successfully restrained.

The researcher, like the master artist discovers the intrinsic authenticity of a subject to the degree that the human, singular identity engages a phenomenon immediately without the mediation and oblique approach of reason and sentiment. Thereby, through immediacy, the human quintessence recognizes the essential significance of an object. Thus, in present timing, through direct cognition, a phenomenon is experienced as it exists intrinsically.

The materialist, claiming an exclusively, physical perspective as sufficient evidence of reality, is profoundly mistaken. That is, the restricted scrutiny of the merely, superficial features and properties of a phenomenon is too shallow. Consequently, a perspective established upon abstract conceptualization from exclusively physically derived evidence is inadequate because it is founded upon transient information and not intrinsic significance. Therefore, human cognition remains confined and restricted because of a materialistic prejudice of perspective that offers only a superficial view.

Materialism is not confined to the scientist and the philosopher but it is a common fallacy of perception that may be recognized anywhere. Even the spiritualist is convinced of extrasensory matter, imagining a parallel condition of existence composed of rarefied material.

However, when conventional, cognitive approaches are restrained, immediate experience through the aegis of the human, singular identity, reveals a neglected proportion of existence that is composed of qualitatively distinct, intrinsic identities.

Nevertheless, the intrinsic condition of phenomena remains elusive except through direct engagement. It cannot be justified through reason or argument because profundity is either known experientially or it remains undiscovered. Thus, intangible existence remains an incomprehensible condition to the materialistic approach and it cannot be qualified through abstract evaluation.

Never definitive, the reasoned approach only approximates reality. Of necessity, it works obliquely and, ideally, calculates physical properties that can be quantified and, consequently, justified mathematically. Otherwise, the intellect proceeds logically endeavoring to comprehend through systematic argument. However, the properties that are capable of being reduced into numerical terms or logically argued are necessarily physical in nature. Thus, we surmise and deduce the nature of existence based upon superficial appearances and not intrinsic content.

Obviously, it is unsatisfactory to settle for partial and superficial knowledge when it is possible to experience the qualitatively distinct, intrinsic identity of a phenomenon directly and discover it for what it inherently is. At fault here is a prejudice in favor of an exclusively materialistic perspective and concomitant ignorance concerning the existence of an approach that is direct and immediate. Consequently, human existential understanding is insufficient and our philosophy vague.

The capacity of direct cognition resides with the human intrinsic significance. The human ipseity recognizes the similarly, incorporeal identities that essentially epitomize other people and all other phenomena. Thus, we enter into a dimension populated with distinct entities, and we recognize them for their qualitative uniqueness. Thereby, we have left our former superficial evaluation of the phenomenal world, exclusively founded upon physical properties, forever behind us. We no longer evaluate phenomena abstractly and indirectly but we find them essentially distinguishable.

Observation becomes direct cognition when the human, essential identity immediately engages a phenomenon. Unfortunately, a mentality, prejudiced in favor of the exclusive significance of appearances, cannot proceed further because the identity of the human being is deemed, material. Thus, the human intrinsic identity that we describe as incorporeally extant, will be denied existence. Consequently, we cannot determine the incorporeal existence of phenomena because intangible realities, known through direct cognition by the human essence, are unrecognizable through a materialistic approach that only acknowledges and addresses physical appearances.

Alike to materialistic exclusivity, all pre-conceptual constructions are similarly recognized as positions of prejudice. Specialization according to select scholarship merely hinders original knowledge that would otherwise directly arise through immediate engagement. Thus, the astrophysicist regards the firmament from the narrowness of the laws of physics and interprets observations accordingly, revealing an incomprehensible universe wherein mathematical agility and hypothetical manipulation supersede essential distinctions.

The human essence is of a caliber that fathoms incorporeal significances. It discerns the qualitatively distinct, intrinsic identity of phenomena to be as important as solid matter and even more impressive because the obvious, physical appearance is recognized as superficial while the authentic identity is discovered to be essential. That is to say, the human, cerebral faculty does not possess this ability but the intrinsic human identity does.

There is no developmental value to us if the

experience of the human, essential identity remains the conclusion of our researches because our progress does not rest with eccentricity however profound our understanding may be. Rather, the perspective of the human essential identity, established upon a position of absolute authenticity, provides a means whereby phenomena may be intrinsically identified. Knowledge of the essential identity allows us to move away from materialism, and an exclusively intellectual and emotional evaluation of life, to a condition of cognitive immediacy.

As the legitimate identity of the human being, the essential distinction has the capacity to recognize the singular significance of itself and other phenomena. The human essence is incorporeal, not biological, and it is consequently responsive to intangible distinctions. Therefore, upon direct engagement it discerns the intrinsic existence of other people and of phenomenal appearances.

The consequence of an experiential recognition of the human, incorporeal constitution is the establishment of our essential significance as the legitimate identity of the human being. Secure in its position as sovereign authority, the essence achieves knowledge concerning other essentials because it is similarly elemental. Thus, four specific results accrue from self-identification. The direct, experiential cognition of our own unique individuality; the identification of the same intrinsic existence of others; the discovery of the qualitatively distinct, essential identity of phenomena; and, immediate experiential knowledge concerning the significance of these things. These are all conspicuous realities, yet they remain unrecognized by the materialistic mentality because they lack physical significance.

Unfortunately, the soul of the human being as the feeling sentient nature, often remains at odds with the new arrangement. In this sense there exists a conflict between a former mentality and that which is required to allow the human being to develop towards a cognitively autonomous condition.

There are those who seek to dismiss this conflict altogether and imagine that our continued development is assured through a routine of techniques, practices and exercises. Others confuse the exigency of rejuvenation with the mystical approach that requires a prolonged preoccupation with an ephemeral experience. The calming effect is thought to influence and dissipate the imbalances of the human psyche and thereby establish a condition of existential liberty.

The reality is that the human being has no significant future except through the establishment of a rejuvenated disposition. Otherwise the consequences of a malignant and self-defeating, emotional constitution is a regression towards an increasingly virulent materialism or its polar opposite, which is escapism of one kind or another. In fact, it is the moment by moment challenges that reveal the shortcomings of our mentality and offer practical opportunities to allow counter-productive behaviors to be superseded by approaches that have a more realistic future.

The human psyche needs to be wholesomely reestablished to a condition that is appropriate to a destiny of mature liberty. This requires that our former mentality be relinquished for one that is a suitable complement to autonomy and liberation. Our existing mentality is insufficient to the task.

The attainment of a reworked psychology requires the examination of behaviors and attitudes. However, this is not merely time consuming introspection but requires willing relinquishment of obviously unsustainable proclivities. But the transformation of the psyche is unachievable through our own capacity because we do not possess the necessary successor to our old disposition. Consequently, a realistic transformation requires that the individual permit the direct influence upon the heart, of Virtue, in order that Virtue may establish an appropriately wholesome condition of soul. In other words, the reestablishment of the human psyche upon an entirely regenerated basis is essential. There is nothing of value in a mentality of egotism, anxiety and resentment. It needs to be shed, or there is no prospect of a meaningful future.

An openness of heart is required because the heart is crucial in terms of the psyche. Nevertheless, there is no contradiction between the recognition of the essence of the human constitution and the regenerative experience of Virtue upon the soul. On the contrary, the immediate experience of a qualitatively distinct, intangible existence assures us of the authenticity of our approach, whereby in confidence we surrender the refashioning the human, feeling-sentient nature, to Virtue. Indeed, it is in this sense that surrender is entirely justified.

Sincerity of heart is expedient to soul transformation. Thereby, we immediately experience the distinction of Virtue, but it is not required that we define it. In fact it is better that we do not. Virtue, alike to other qualitatively distinct, intrinsic identities is only determined for its authenticity, experientially. It remains unknown through abstract conceptualization.

The regeneration of the soul is not achieved through religious practices and disciplines that have become rote and without immediate significance. The approach is sincerity and willingness while Virtue suitably restructures our souls according to the prerequisites of a meaningful future of sovereign autonomy. It is essential that these steps be taken otherwise the old disposition prevents the progression and development of the human being towards an autonomous and emancipated existence. Everything else of significance follows upon the renewal of our psyche.

Sincerity and open-heartedness, whereby Virtue may rebuild our mentality, is vital. Otherwise, nothing really happens in terms of the human being because the crux of the qualitative development of the soul concerns an ethical disposition.

When the heart is open to Virtue, what occurs to the soul is profoundly significant. The heart is rendered vulnerable which is the vital prerequisite of change. This provides access to our temperamental disposition wherein lies our frailty.

Much distress lingers in the present from times gone by. These too are successfully addressed when vividly recalled and experienced anew in order that they can be finally relinquished. However, effective reconstruction of the soul only occurs through the aegis of Virtue. There is nothing in the human, established constitution that is capable rebuilding the soul in a manner appropriate to a future condition of meaningful liberty. That is because the human disposition requires an entirely new and unjaded, archetypal mien. The old is unsuited to a substantive and emancipated future because it will only perpetuate an existence, different in form may be, but reminiscent of the same bondage. The old archetype was sufficient for the superficial human being but is inadequate for the essential person.

25. ETHICAL REESTABLISHMENT

The human singularity recognizes its distinct existence and the human constitution becomes reoriented upon the significant foundation of its authentic identity. This is a considerable improvement over the former misconception that reduced the human identity to an organism or one of its various functions. Upon this new basis the human being is able to distinguish between reality and conjecture because intrinsic identity exists in a condition readily accessible to the human, essential identity. The former practice of indirect evaluation was incapable of knowing anything definitively but the human essence, as intransient and incorporeal, engages only the essential significance of phenomena.

The human essence is known through immediate engagement to be absolutely authentic. But its essential existence is physically unjustified and, consequently, an exclusively materialistic mentality is incapable of acknowledging it. Nevertheless, the justification for the existence of the human essence is independent of reasoning. It must self-recognize, experientially without reference to conjecture, calculation or argument. Neither do sentimental preferences influence its acknowledgment.

Recognizing the authentic identity of someone else is similarly immediate and experiential. But it requires a significantly distinct dynamic. It is scarcely possible to discern the essential existence of someone else if we remain preoccupied with ourselves. The identity of another person must be approached in the same direct manner whereby we acknowledge our own essence. This required the setting aside of all preconceptions and sentiments. The difference in determining the significance of someone else, however, is that our attention must be exclusively concerned with the inherence of the other person. In order to recognize their significance it no longer matters what happen to ourselves. Our own self becomes of marginal importance and thereby we encounter the you of another. Thus, we meet the other person in a condition of their authentic existence and find that only by removing attention from ourselves do we discover them. This is a deeply moving experience of tremendous significance and may be subsequently described as authentic love.

We do not discover the essential significance and intrinsic identities of things through conventional cognition. All the scholarship in the world cannot achieve definitive knowledge. Yet, the apparent mysteries encountered through standard perception are solved through the immediate encounter because thereby the essential existence of things becomes known.

The pedestrian approach requires thorough research into the opinions and orthodox interpretations of prior erudition, in order to determine the identity of a phenomenon. It is imagined that definitive knowledge may be achieved through the authority of pre-conceptual accumulation. Thereby, orthodoxy is only accorded to the most rigorous and convincing argument and further determined by peer consensus. This is the extent of the jurisdiction of conventional authority.

However, there is no such thing as definitive proof through argument unless it addresses a mathematical scenario. But mathematics of itself has no intrinsic identity. It is either an abstract conceptualization of unidimensional situations, or it exists as relationships between solely the quantifiable aspects of physical properties. Indeed, however carefully and explicitly structured a mathematical argument may be, it never approaches experientially derived knowledge because the one deals with the relationships of quantities, while direct cognition addresses actual existence.

In a similar manner, abstract rationalism attempts to determine the identity of a phenomenon through the enumeration of the similar properties of something previously established. The intellect is incapable of direct identification, but it must always associate the new with prior conceptualization. It cannot definitively identify, but it merely evaluates through deliberation and estimation.

That is to say, the intellect possesses indirectly assessed knowledge and functions in the abstract, remotely from the incident. This is insufficient because conclusions always remain indefinite. In order that the inherence of phenomena may be recognized, a direct experience is essential. Thus, things become known for their essential identities and not merely on the basis of their superficial and intellectually manageable properties.

Intrinsic singularities are discovered when the human, essential identity engages an object immediately. Unlike the intellect, the human essence is an identity. It dwells in a condition in which only the profound proportion of phenomena is discerned. Therefore, being essential and original, the human, identity recognizes the similarly, intrinsic dimension that underlies appearances. Consequently, the human, incorporeal quintessence does not assess things through indirect evaluation nor by calculation and association. It engages phenomena immediately, solely upon the basis of their intrinsic existence.

The human essence only recognizes unequivocal authenticity and it does so through the immediacy of one absolute, engaging with another. Predictably, the absolute and incorporeal identity of the human distinction is of the same existence as the definitive identity of other phenomena.

Through direct cognition, phenomena, including the human, individual identity, are immediately engaged and recognized for their intrinsic significance. The human essence looks to others and recognizes the authenticity of their singular existence. Thereby, we become increasingly familiar with the tenor of something in its essential condition, and we are able to determine the authentic from the contrived.

A glimpse of the essential existence of phenomena offers us a tantalizing preview of a more significant human future than that presented through the narrow view of an exclusively materialistic, philosophical perspective. However, we recognize that the disposition of our human psyche remains ill equipped for a future of the tenor that we have experienced through direct cognition. It is established upon a cumulative heritage of self-survival and ignorance and our present mentality hinders our progress towards an autonomous condition of existence. Yet, we do not possess an appropriate replacement of the caliber of maturity necessary for us to attain our potential destiny as entirely emancipated human beings.

But the successor disposition of soul is attainable through the aegis of Virtue. It requires that we do our part and, through open-heartedness, allow Virtue to transform the old condition and establish the new. Once again, as with all matters involving qualitatively distinct, intrinsic identities, Virtue is only recognized experientially and our experience of it must remain uninfluenced by our subjective evaluation. That is to say, we must allow the principle of Virtue to be what it really is.

The human, essential identity is known through immediate engagement. Thereby, we recognize the reality of our own existence. This direct knowledge has an uplifting effect upon the soul and encourages us considerably.

In terms of profundity, there is no physical space that enables us to distinguish between one essential distinction and another. Intrinsic identities are found to be distinct through the direct experience of the individual significance of their existence.

Virtue is also experientially known to be extant and is distinguished in the same qualitative way that other essential distinctions are differentiated. Virtue, as an extant entity, is recognized to be of a similar substance as the human essence while remaining distinctly particular. That is to say, the principle of Virtue is distinguished from our own singularity through the inherent originality of its particular existence.

Thus, in the same manner whereby phenomena are immediately approached in order to be known intrinsically; Virtue is similarly experienced without reference to our own conceptualization and consequently, known for its authenticity through immediate engagement.

Virtue is known to be real and identified as singular through immediate engagement. The soul of the human being approaches Virtue immediately, through sincerity. We do not endeavor to identify incorporeal realities through reason, sentimental preference or by association with a preconceived notion. We merely experience them. We are disinterested in what we think or imagine Virtue to be but desire Virtue to be what it authentically is. If Virtue were merely as we imagined then it would possess little influence upon our preconditioned mentality. Virtue is significant to us because through the original condition of its existence, our future becomes established in the present, through its mandate.

Thus, the possibility of a vastly more significant prospect is established as if it were a completely new existence. The old mentality very obviously, cannot take us any further towards a wholesome destiny but merely promises us more of the same. That is why it is essential that we willingly relinquish it. Virtue makes this transformation of soul a reality. Virtue, in this sense, is the epitome of our potential destiny.

The human essence experiences the intrinsic identity of things and knows them immediately as reality, by means of the direct approach. But the human soul approaches Virtue through the heart and the soul. Through the aegis of Virtue, the soul is thereby reestablished upon a wholesome foundation. If one desires to approach Virtue, no ritual, ceremony, incantation or verbiage can substitute for the condition of sincerity and open-heartedness. The heart is the portal of ingress and egress whereby the human soul is opened to Virtue and renewed.

Virtue must be approached with a sincerity void of the myriad counterfeit sentiments and posturing that merely clutter our view. The human soul engages Virtue modestly, and no other approach is appropriate. Thereby, we avoid reducing our immediate experience into our own conceptual terms and merely imagining an event while none has actually taken place. In fact, resistance to the frequent practice of imagining a so-called spiritual experience or pretending to know something that is otherwise elusive, is a significant justification for the materialistic position. The materialist is anxious less we relinquish the exclusively, physical approach that seems substantial, for a delusion. But the materialistic philosophy itself does not hold up to severe scrutiny either.

The materialistic stance is an understandable reaction to a long history of unfounded belief and superstition. We wish to establish a cognitive position towards existence that is readily verifiable and demonstrably authentic, and conceptualization established upon physical evidence seems entirely reasonable. But the physical properties of phenomena are merely the superficial components. Identity does not reside in the physical but in the intrinsic condition.

The intrinsic condition of a phenomenon is distinguished by its qualitative distinction. But the qualitative distinction is intangible and cannot be discerned in terms of the physical properties. Thus, a philosophy of life founded upon exclusively physical evidence is an abstract construction. In reality, there is no physical evidence without intrinsic identity because the appearance is a consequence of absolute existence. Thus, the existence of something is not dependent upon its dimensions or any other physical circumstances because properties cannot exist upon their own.

The abstract approach that attributes autonomous existence to physical conditions is similarly faulted wherever it is assumed that the tangible appearance alone possess independent continuance. Physical properties represent a facet of a whole phenomena that predominantly includes the substantive. Their dimensions and the forces acting upon them have no independent existence separate from the intrinsic identity of the entire object itself. In this regard, the theoretical sciences that manipulate the values of physical properties independently of the significance of an actual phenomenon, as if the conclusions of their appraisal possessed intrinsic identity, is bound to reveal a peculiar and distorted version of reality.

The entire approach we are proposing, however, commences with the establishment of a direct cognition towards ourselves and other phenomena that is both immediate and experiential. We recognize the shortcomings of the merely, material perspective and the contrived manner whereby qualitative distinctions are dismissed in theory yet, embraced in practice. The materialistic perspective is contradictory in that, while it denies incorporeal reality, it must recognize intangible significances experientially, in everyday life. Existence without the qualitative dimension would be an untenable situation, remote from reality. In fact, if the abstract, materialistically founded conceptualization of existence were for one moment imagined as authentic, the resultant image would not resemble our experience of life because it would a supposition devoid of significance.

An experientially established recognition of the qualitative dimension of existence, through immediate engagement by the human essential singularity, provides a foundation whereupon the intangible nature of existence can be further explored. This should not be a hard concept to grasp because, for example, the human, emotional condition is similarly intangible yet, its existence is thoroughly qualified through experience alone.

The human soul-disposition determines the quality of our interactions with others, the manner whereby we engage the circumstances and challenge of life, and also our own state of mind. The one individual address a situation differently from another depending on their particular demeanor and consequent, idiosyncrasy of approach.

The psyche exists in circumstances that are distinctly different from the condition of our human, essential identity. The realm of emotionality is readily influenced by those same compulsions that operate in the animal kingdom, with the added confusion of our inherent yearning for autonomous existence.

The human being, ignorant of the significance of an extant incorporeal dimension and preoccupied with superficial properties as if they possessed separate existence, identifies with the condition of mortality. However, reason and an inherent yearning for autonomous existence prevent the complete subjection of the human soul by the animal nature. But the demands of the animal nature and their ramifications are promoted by similar influences that serve the animal kingdom in the necessities of survival and adaption. These are extant intangible propensities, appetites, tempers and passions that are ascribed instinctual status and reveal the temperamental distinction of the animal. However, their dominance is inappropriate to the human condition because they deter us from our destiny of sovereign autonomy. They hound humanity according to their particular proclivity. In animals they are differentiated by the particular disposition of the creature. Indeed, all human excesses may be found epitomized within the dominant character of different animal species.

While the demeanor of the animal influences its form and its appropriateness to an optimum ecological niche, the inherited and developed propensities of the human psyche may or may not serve to advantage. Nevertheless, bondage to a mentality that prevents further progress towards human, maturity is assuaged through the aegis of Virtue. That is to say, the soul becomes reestablished to the degree that the human heart engages Virtue in complete sincerity.

Virtue is experientially recognized for the singularity and quality of its existence. But incorporeal significances cannot be articulated in the same manner in which physical appearances are readily justified. They have neither measure nor dimension according to which they may be defined and classified. They must be distinguished by their qualitative nature and known for their intrinsic singularity.

The identity of Virtue is experienced as a singularity of sovereign autonomy and astonishing stature. We recognize an extant individuality that ensouls ideals and qualities alike to a new human archetype. However, the only manner whereby the human constitution may be equipped for a similar destiny is through a comprehensive reorientation of soul. Yet, it is for Virtue to establish the new condition within us because we do not possess it and cannot readily conceive of it. Nevertheless, Virtue of itself embodies it.

The virtues of the Greek philosophers were Restraint, Wisdom, Justice and Courage. These, together with the theological virtues may be considered expressions of the archetypal ideal, which is Virtue itself.

The manner whereby incorporeal identities are most appropriately articulated, is art. The artist experiences an intangible quality and endeavors to communicate its authenticity through the metaphoric description of a particular medium. Virtue has been represented artistically since classical times as separately revered natures and venerated as the qualities of the Gods, seemingly unreachable to human striving. But now they are attainable to human kind as we journey onward towards a more meaningful future.

345

THE MEANINGFUL VOLUME OF EXISTENCE
An Exploration of the Overlooked Intangible Significance of Phenomena

THE OBSOLETE SELF
Individual Uniqueness and Significance beyond Egocentrism

HUMAN SOVEREIGN AUTONOMY
The Discovery of the Human Ipseity and its Establishment as the Essential Authority of the Human Constitution

THE TRANSFORMATION OF THE SOUL
From Self-Centeredness to Sovereign Autonomy

THE IMPLICATION OF HUMAN, INCORPOREAL EXISTENCE
The Overlooked Significance of the Intangible and Qualitative Dimension of Existence

IMMEDIATE EXPERIENTIAL COGNITION
The Inherent Human Capacity of Immediate Engagement

THE HUMAN ESSENTIAL IDENTITY
Direct Experience of Intangible Significance

KNOWLEDGE THROUGH DIRECT COGNITION
The Human Conscious Individuality and Immediately Experienced Reality

www.ingramcontent.com/pod-product-compliance
Lightning Source LLC
Chambersburg PA
CBHW060242100426
42742CB00011B/1611